PUBLISHING
with
CD-ROM

A Guide to Compact Disc
Optical Storage Technologies
for Providers of
Publishing Services

Patti Myers

MECKLER PUBLISHING CORPORATION
IN ASSOCIATION WITH
THE NATIONAL COMPOSITION ASSOCIATION

Other NCA Books by Patti Myers:

Telecommunicating for Typesetting

Typesetting From Magnetic Media

ISBN 088736-181-1
Meckler Publishing Corporation
in association with
The National Composition Association

The manuscript for this book was prepared originally on a personal computer with the XyWrite word processing program. The XyWrite files, left in ASCII format, had generic codes embedded within the text to indicate font styles and heads. These files were sent on disk from the author to NCA headquarters in Arlington, Virginia, where the files were further prepared for translation into typographic formatting. The manuscript was typeset by Robey Graphics, Inc., of Washington, DC, where the files were run through additional coding translations and processed on a CCI 400 front-end system and output to a Linotron 202. The book was set in the Optima family of typefaces.

BOOK ORGANIZATION

This book is organized into five major sections.

Section 1 defines optical storage and its various forms. Each type of optical storage media is explained, highlighting their similarities, differences and uses. This forms a framework for understanding optical technology and all forms of optical storage.

Section 2 describes the various ways CD-ROMs are being used today and what materials have thus far been published and distributed on CD-ROMs.

Section 3 explores the publishing of a CD-ROM. Included are considerations that go into creating a CD-ROM title, the exact steps of producing a disc, and the systems/services for CD-ROM creation.

Section 4 puts a perspective on the future of CD-ROMs and its implications for the providers of publishing and information services.

Section 5 is a collection of references: a glossary of CD-ROM terminology, a reading list on CD-ROM (for those interested in further information), and a listing of companies involved in various CD-ROM activities.

Many of the technical descriptions about CD-ROM and optical storage can be found in figure captions and information boxes.

ACKNOWLEDGMENTS

The author would like to thank Judith Paris Roth for her support and assistance. Besides providing background materials and reading a preliminary draft of the manuscript, her suggestions and encouragement were so very helpful and appreciated.

The author would also like to acknowledge the vision of the National Composition Association (NCA), its staff, and William A. Hohns, Chairman of the NCA Board of Directors. Their foresight about the role of optical publishing allowed this book to be planned and scheduled for timely publication. Several recent articles (including one appearing in *Time* the same week this manuscript was being submitted) illustrate how well they have anticipated and provided for NCA members' need to know about new publishing trends and opportunities.

TABLE OF CONTENTS

INTRODUCTION

As I write this book I am surrounded by information. There are stocks of materials (to be read and/or filed), bookshelves filled with reference materials, the bookcase dedicated to software manuals, large file cabinets containing various types of documentation, and the personal computer on my desk—visa to my local electronic storage and to distant online databases.

This environment points out a number of information handling problems. All this information takes up so much space! The ability to locate data on a given topic depends not only on a good filing system. Locating what I want is a function of my ability to figure out *where* it's filed. The aforementioned sentence might imply everything is constantly organized in files (which, of course, is not the case). Another problem is the difficulty of locating all information that might be relevant. In the file cabinet labeled 'Local Area Networks' are, to be sure, numerous materials related to the topic. And I have a book on the subject. It's not on the bookshelf, though, since an associate borrowed it. There's also revelant data in notes and proceedings from a new-technologies conference last month. And didn't someone mention a recent article in a major publication describing a new breakthrough which would completely change existing LAN dogma?

There is no doubt we can all relate similar information handling problems. In industries like ours where so much change occurs at such a rapid rate, keeping track of relevant information (let alone up to date information) is not easy. In recent years both the trade and popular press have written a great deal about new technologies and trends related to printing and publishing. In articles and speeches, many advances receive 'the Gutenberg invocation' (with gems such as "not since Gutenberg invented moveable type has a publishing process so advanced been introduced" "bye, bye Gutenberg", and the like). Such rhetoric has been applied to CRT typesetters, laser printers, interactive pagination systems, desktop publishing and others.

Two new, hot topics causing a lot of excitement are 'optical publishing' and something called a CD-ROM (Compact Disc-Read Only Memory). No matter how inaccurate, confusing or incomplete the description and cited significance are, the articles describe this latest phenomenon in glowing terms. Will CD-ROM—that magical tiny disc that can hold 600 megabytes of information—be the answer to our information handling dreams? Some say it will.

The purpose of this book is to explore that question with a concise, relevant introduction to CD-ROM and optical publishing. The book won't take up too much space on your bookshelf, yet it has the basics you need to understand what CD-ROM is all about.

As with all new technologies, a variety of diverse claims may be applied (correctly or incorrectly) to one product, when in fact they might actually apply to several products, to another product, or to none. One of the goals of this book is to clarify exactly what CD-ROM is and isn't.

Since the first commercially-available optical disc product appeared, some products have not been gigantic commercial successes. Technological advances made other, more viable products and processes possible. Also during that time, more people became aware of optical discs. Some know a lot about one kind of optical disc, but little about other versions. Terms used by one may have different meaning to another. Another goal is to provide a framework for understanding the use and differences in optical discs and optical publishing terminology.

Since my introduction to optical disc technology in 1978, I have been fascinated by its potential—not in the 'tech-y' sense, but in how it could relate to me as the user. Our plan is to relate CD-ROM to you and your business.

Another goal is to provide answers to questions you might have as you are reading about CD-ROM. What does one need to use a CD-ROM? How much does a CD-ROM cost to make? How much does someone pay to use a CD-ROM? How are CD-ROMs being used now? How will they be used in the future? What's involved in creating a CD-ROM? How 'solid' is the technology? What companies are actively involved with CD-ROM?

Before we go any further, let's begin with an obvious question: why should you want to know about CD-ROM?

FIVE REASONS TO KNOW MORE ABOUT CD-ROM

1. CD-ROM will have some impact on your business.

2. Your company/department may find it applicable for some production operations and some managment applications.

3. As a provider of publishing and/or information services, your clients will—at the very least—probably consider publishing on CD-ROM at some time in the future (if they haven't already). To continue to provide clients with publishing services, you'll need to know the implications of CD-ROM on manuscript preparation, data capture, image digitizing, and more.

4. CD-ROM publishing requires special expertise. Perhaps CD-ROM will be a new area in which your company/department can expand.

5. Knowing more about CD-ROM and optical publishing you'll be able to impress (and perhaps fascinate) friends, relatives, and business associates with your wisdom and ability to keep current on relevant trends and breakthroughs.

SECTION 1

OPTICAL STORAGE: DEFINING A FAMILY OF PRODUCTS

Optical storage (also referred to as *optical memory*) is the term used to distinguish media using laser optics (versus magnetic or other technology) for reading and/or storing data. Optical storage media come in a variety of shapes and sizes (3½", 4.72", 5¼", 8" and 12" flat disks, and credit-size cards) and are surrounded by a colorful assortment of acronyms (all of which are defined in the glossary at the back of the book). For example:

WORM
DRAW
OD3 (pronounced *o-dee-cubed*)
CD-ROM (pronounced *see-dee-rom*)
CD-I(pronounced *see-dee-eye*)
CD-PROM(pronounced *see-dee-prom*)
CD-EPROM(pronounced *see-dee-ee-prom*)
OROM (pronounced *o-rom*)
M-0 (pronounced *em-o*)

While the focus of this publication is primarily the form known as CD-ROM, an orientation[1] to all optical storage variations is beneficial.

COMMON FAMILY TRAITS

A laser beam is responsible for originally recording data for optical storage media. A laser beam is also responsible for reading data from all optical media.

Because the laser beam can focus within a much smaller area than a magnetic reading/writing mechanism, optical storage media can store much more data than magnetic media. The tracks can be much closer together than tracks in magnetic media. (For example, one version of optical disc has almost 16,000 tracks per inch (tpi). In comparison, floppy disks are usually 96 tpi or less and Winchester disks are several hundred tpi). The combination of closely-packed tracks and tiny bit elements yields significant compact storage potential for all members of the optical storage family. Figure 4 lists the storage capacity for various storage media.

---

[1] The reader will no doubt notice the disc/disk spelling variations. The disc (with a C) spelling is to differeniate optical platters from magnetic disks (with a K).

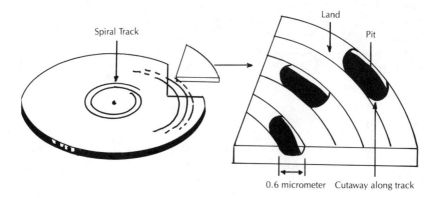

CD ROM

Spiral Track

CUTAWAY ALONG TRACK

Land

Pit

0.6 micrometer   Cutaway along track

SIDE VIEW OF TRACK

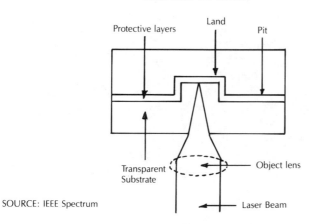

Protective layers

Land

Pit

Transparent
Substrate

Object lens

SOURCE: IEEE Spectrum

Laser Beam

FIGURE 1:

Optical Storage Technology

All optical media store data as indentations ('pits' and 'lands' or bubbles/puddles) along tracks in the medium. The tracks are encased in protective layers and a transparent substrate. A laser beam, focused through a lensing mechanism, detects the indentations and their binary value. Within the reading mechanism, the combination of 0s and 1s is interpreted into data (either analog or digital) representations for use with computer, audio and/or video components. The interpretation may be converting the pattern in terms of the transition from a land to a pit or a pit to a land (as a '1') and the run length between transitions (as a 0). Or, for some forms of optical storage, the interpretation is of the magnetic value (zero or one) of the indentation. The nature of the interpretation depends on which optical medium is being read.

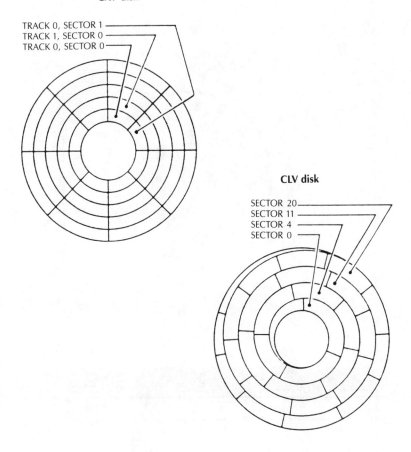

CAV disk

TRACK 0, SECTOR 1
TRACK 1, SECTOR 0
TRACK 0, SECTOR 0

CLV disk

SECTOR 20
SECTOR 11
SECTOR 4
SECTOR 0

FIGURE 2:

Tracks on a Storage Disc

Tracks can be either a series of concentric circles or one continuous tight spiral. Those disks with concentric circles/tracks revolve at a fixed rate of speed and require a reader/player which supports CAV (constant angular velocity). Those with one continuous sprial track contain more sectors at the outer edges, while those with concentric tracks have the same number of sectors per track, regardless of track location.

Those with one continuous spiral track require more sophisticated speeding up and slowing down as they rotate to supply a constant data rate for proper reading. They require readers/players which support CLV (constant linear velocity) in order to maintain a constant data rate.

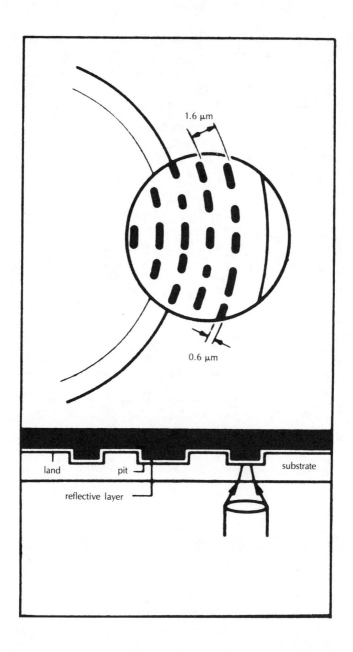

FIGURE 3:

Pits and Lands

In addition to very small spacing between tracks, the pits are very small (less than 0.6 micrometers in width and up to 3.3 micrometers in length). To give some tangible way of relating to size, consider that a width of 300 pits is not quite as wide as the thickness of a single human hair! The density of pits/lands yields almost 25,000 bpi of linear data density, or the equivalent of 2 billion bits!!

FIGURE 4
Storage Capacity for Various Media

Type of Media	Size	Capacity
OPTICAL		
Write-Once Disk	12"	1,300-4,000 MB
Write-Once Disk	5¼"	250-500 MB
Eraseable Disk	5¼"	300-800 MB
OROM Disk	5¼"	500-1,000 MB
CD-ROM	4.72"	550-600 MB
MAGNETIC		
Floppy Disk	5¼"	0.3 MB
Winchester-type Disk	5¼"	10-20 MB
Magnetic Hard Disk		80-300 MB
1600 bpi Mag Tape		25 MB

Another common characteristic of all members of the optical storage family are the special requirements for the reader/player. In addition to a laser reading mechanism, the player must allow for different physical properties, such as disc size, the way a disc is sectored, density of tracks, etc. This situation is somewhat analogous to disk drive variations for various types of magnetic media.

Optical storage media, unlike magnetic media, is not affected by magnetic fields, dust, moisture, ballpoint pens, rough handling, etc. Once optical media has been encoded with data, protective layers provide a virtual shield against damage or corruption of the data. However, in writing data onto the optical storage media a specific, super-clean environment is mandatory. Due to the microscopic size of the data elements, even minute imperfections in the medium or particles in the environment can introduce faulty storage or read errors.

Another common characteristic is a requirement for error-checking schemes to insure data is accurately written, read and interpreted. The level of error checking and correction varies among members of the optical storage family.

THE GENEALOGY OF OPTICAL STORAGE MEDIA

With these common characteristics in mind, we can now turn to the differences in optical storage media. The most meaningful way to categorize optical media is by primary purpose. There are three basic families of optical memory:

READ ONLY MEMORY (ROM)—for distributing large and specialized kinds of data and materials.

WRITE-ONLY MEMORY—for a permanent storage of data, without the ability to write-over or delete data once it is placed on the media.

ERASABLE MEMORY—for storage of large volumes of data, with the ability to write over data on the media; seen as a perpherial component, like magnetic disk drives, in computer operations.

Each family is divided into two major households based on two primary types of signals: digital and analog. Digital signals are binary (off/on; black/white; 1s and 0s). Analog signals are more variable (many shades of gray versus black-and-white; a range of tones; colors, etc.). Analog signals, like voice communications or broadcast television, is represented in variable length elements. Each family member can handle, in some fashion, both types of signals. However, their primary use (and usually more efficient use) is in handling one type of data signal or the other.

THE ROM FAMILY

All members of the ROM family serve as information delivery vehicles. They are the means of presenting data (in the form of sound, text, images, motion pictures, even computer programs) to numerous end users. In each case, multiple copies have been mass-produced either through a stamping procedure (to mold the *pits* and *lands* into the discs) or through injection molding.

Because they are mass-produced, ROM media can be an economical way to distribute large amounts of information.

To read ROM media a low-powered laser beam is used. The player will also contain hardware and, in some cases, software to perform the necessary level of read error checking and interpretation of stored data.

Members of the ROM-Analog Household

Videodiscs are 12″ platters—about the size of record albums, only thicker. Their major function is to store audio, still frames and/or motion sequences. A videodisc can store up to 54,000 single frames, the equivalent of:
— 54,000 slides
— 60 minutes of motion sequences
— 1 billion bytes of digital data (expressed in analog form).

In addition, a videodisc has two sound tracks which can be used simultaneously or separately. Most often, the majority of the videodisc is used for image storage and accompanying audio with some digital data about the location and sequencing of frames.

The general public became aware of videodiscs when RCA attempted to sell videodisc-versions of movies, how-to guides, and other general interest programs, such as NFL highlights. As an alternative to lower-priced, erasable/reuseable videotapes, consumer videodiscs were not a commercial success.

Where videodiscs offer unique and powerful benefits are in informational kiosks (like the information booths at Disneyland) and in instruc-

FIGURE 5:

Optical Storage Genealogy

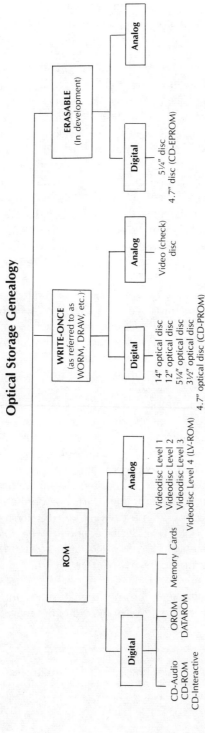

ROM

Digital
- CD-Audio
- CD-ROM
- CD-Interactive

OROM
DATAROM
Memory Cards

Analog
- Videodisc Level 1
- Videodisc Level 2
- Videodisc Level 3
- Videodisc Level 4 (LV-ROM)

WRITE-ONCE
(as referred to as WORM, DRAW, etc.)

Digital
- 14" optical disc
- 12" optical disc
- 5¼" optical disc
- 3½" optical disc
- 4.7" optical disc (CD-PROM)
- Memory Cards

Analog
- Video (check) disc

ERASABLE
(In development)

Digital
- 5¼" disc
- 4.7" disc (CD-EPROM)

Analog

ROM Household Traits
- Recorded prior to distribution
- Uses popular manufacturing technique for mass reproduction
- Uses standard players
- Cannot be erased or written upon
- Inexpensive media

Write-Once Household Traits
- On-site recording/writing
- Uses custom drives
- Less density (bytes/inch) than ROM
- Probably less density than Erasable
- Cannot be erased after writing

Common Traits for All Families
- Laser read & written
- Low cost storage
- Compact storage
- High-density storage
- Removable and transportable
- Durable

Erasable Household Traits
- Writing/recording on site
- Erasing/rewriting on site
- Unproven technology
- Less density (bytes/inch) than ROM

tional/training applications. In each case, the videodisc has the ability to quickly and selectively follow any number of information paths—including selective audio and visual in different languages, different levels of expertise, different ways of illustrating or expressing a point or concept. Most videodiscs are not played as one continuous serial program. Instead, based on user answers, directions, or preset options, the appropriate 'next' frame—regardless of its physical location on the videodisc—is accessed.[2] This can yield thousands of different sequences and hours of informational or training material, all suited to the individual needs of the user. Today hundreds of videodisc-based programs have been developed for such diverse applications as personnel training; simulation of military equipment operations; handling medical emergencies; helping shoppers select gifts suited for the characteristics of gift-recipient and within the shopper's price range; learning about a museum's collection; and language training.

The videodisc stores analog signals, like the data transmitted for television broadcast. Therefore, videodisc is quite efficient in storing images.

To read/use the information of a videodisc requires a videodisc player. There are four kinds of players, to match the types of data stored on the videodisc and how the disc is to be used.

Level 1 players are for playing consumer videodiscs containing one hour of continuous programs (like films or TV). The major task of the Level 1 players is to read and convert the stored analog signals into video images for display on a television monitor and sounds from the audio soundtracks.

Level 2 videodiscs are interactive videodiscs containing a small amount of digital instruction code as well as analog images and sound. The digital codes are loaded into a RAM chip in the Level 2 player and instruct the player about sequencing and locating different frames on the disc. Level 2 videodiscs and players are used in merchandising and informational kiosks and in educational settings.

Level 3 videodiscs are interactive videodiscs whose programming options are controlled by a separate microcomputer. The microcomputer instructs the videodisc player what frames to read and in what sequence, based on user responses. (The options are usually too many to contain in the memory of a Level 2 player and to write onto the videodisc. The advantage of Level 3 systems is the ability to use the same disc materials with a number of different or changing presentations).

Level 4 videodiscs contain digital data (besides digital instructions) represented as analog signals. The contents of the videodisc may be

---

[2] This ability to present information randomly (versus serially as with magnetic tape or video tape) is called 'interactivity' in the optical world. The term (unlike its use in composition and editing systems to indicate immediate, non-batching processing) comes from the ability of the presentation to 'interact'—based on the user's responses or requests—with the user's level of expertise, information needs, etc.

a combination of video frames, audio and digital data. The Level 4 player works in conjunction with a special controller (to convert analog signals back into digital codes) and a computer which (as in the Level 3 player) instruct the player/drive what portion of the disc to read next. Unfortunately, no standards were established for digital videodiscs. Thus, each Level 4 system works only with videodiscs designed to work with that specific version. As a result, the Level 4 (digital) videodiscs are usually known by brand names (e.g. Laser-Video™, LaserData™, LV-ROM, etc.) from the company who created the disc and the Level 4 player.

While the analog videodisc does a good job of storing and playing back video images, the lack of standard players and encoding formats limit its usefulness outside of specialized fields and applications.

The ROM-Digital Household

The ROM-Digital household has grown rapidly in the past few years, since the very successful introduction of Compact Audio Discs. Unlike its cousin the videodisc where a few hundred copies of a program is a good showing, members of the ROM-Digital household often have thousands of copies and a wide circulation among commercial users or information professionals.

CD-Digital Audio (Compact Disc-Audio) is a 12cm (4.72-inch) disc containing up to 60 minutes of audio. The digital data stored on the disc is converted into analog signals by the CD-Audio player. The CD-Digital Audio player is connected (directly or through a stereo receiver) to stereo speakers. The quick adoption of CD-Audio by consumers is a remarkable phenomenon with over 10 million discs sold within the first three years and over 2,000 different CD-Digital Audio titles produced. The major selling points for CD-Audio are a) its resistance to heat and scratching and b) the clarity and quality of its sound reproduction.

CD-ROM (Compact Disc Read-Only Memory) is a permanent storage medium for large volumes of machine-readable data and/or programs. One disc can hold up to 600 megabytes of information or 15 billion bits of computer data. One CD-ROM disc equals the storage capacity of:

> 150,000 pages (300 books, each with 500 pages)
> 1,500 5¼" floppy disks
> 800 8" floppy disks
> 60 10-MB sealed, Winchester-type disks
> 10 magnetic tapes
> 7.5 80-MB disks
> 2 300-MB disks

CD-ROM's large storage capacity, its permanence, its durability, its portability, its compactness, and its low cost (in comparison with any other digital storage media), make it an ideal medium for economically distributing large amounts of data or programs in machine-readable form. Publishers have already used CD-ROM to publish special collections of journals, encyclopedias, and statistical data along with PC-based software for custom analysis of data.

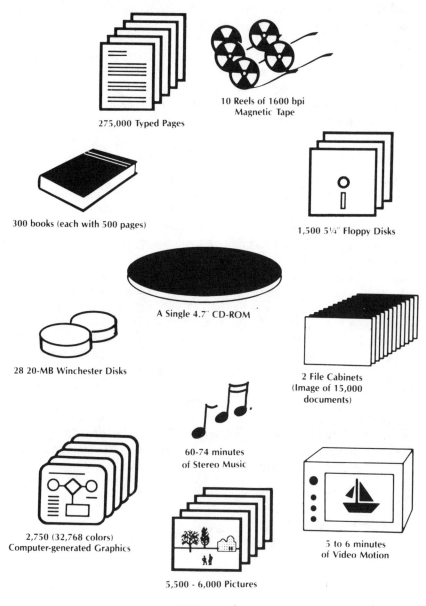

275,000 Typed Pages

10 Reels of 1600 bpi
Magnetic Tape

300 books (each with 500 pages)

1,500 5¼" Floppy Disks

A Single 4.7" CD-ROM

28 20-MB Winchester Disks

2 File Cabinets
(Image of 15,000
documents)

60-74 minutes
of Stereo Music

2,750 (32,768 colors)
Computer-generated Graphics

5,500 - 6,000 Pictures

5 to 6 minutes
of Video Motion

FIGURE 6:

User Data Storage Capacity of a CD-ROM

Because CD-ROM discs deal only in digital information, images and/or audio to accompany text must be expressed in digital form.

Digital information on CD-ROM is read by CD-ROM drives (or players) which, unlike CD-Audio players, transfer the data in digital form directly to a personal or larger computer. Reading accuracy is essential since the loss of one bit can change the meaning of the data. Hence, extensive error-checking and error-correction are required. Standards regarding player/drive tolerances, operational data encoded on CD-ROM discs (to position and control the laser as it reads the disc), the use of CIRC (Cross-Interleaved Reed-Solomon Code) error-control coding, and data structures on CD-ROM discs have been established. These help assure data is correctly read from the disc.

Differing functionality of CD-Audio players and CD-ROM drives means each type of CD disc requires its own type of player/drive. CD drives—like a phonograph player and floppy disc drive—only work with their respective type of media.

Thanks to the physical compatibilities of CD-Audio, CD-ROM, and CD-I discs, the same replication process can be used. However, the 'original' master and formatting of digital data onto a CD-ROM is different from CD-Audio and from CD-I. Thus, replication ('printing') of CD-ROM, CD-I and CD-Audio can be handled by the same manufacturing facility. Yet the preparatory work to create the original requires expertise unique to each type of CD disc.

CD-I (Compact Disc-Interactive) is a new member of the ROM-Digital household. Introduced to the world in early 1986, CD-I discs are expected to become available in late 1987. Like CD-ROM, a CD-I may contain video images, audio, and machine-readable data. Within the player/drive itself will be a microprocessor and programs for rapid random access of data on the disc. Digital data for audio will be converted (as with CD-Audio players) to analog sound for transfer to a stereo amplifier. Other digital data will be directly transferred to a computer and/or video monitor.

In many respects, CD-I is a digital-signal version of a videodisc. Using the CD-I player's built-in microprocessor and memory, a CD-I system is designed to allow users to follow numerous (non-contiguous) paths with rapid transitions from one part of the disc to another (hence the label 'interactive'). However, due to its digital (versus analog) storage technique, CD-I has a limited capacity for image storage and motion sequences. Furthermore, the rotation speed isn't fast enough to access 30 different frames per second for smooth motion. Nevertheless, CD-I offers the possibility of being combined with text-oriented information, visuals and sound to convey the necessary message.

The value of CD-I is not in any additional features over its CD brothers. In fact, only certain types of digital data are permitted on CD-I, while the CD-ROM can store any type of digital data. Instead, the term CD-I is used to designate a compact disc which will be compatible with the capabilities of a new type of compact disc player. (For more on the differences and similarities of CD-Audio, CD-I and CD-ROM, see Figure 7, page 21).

OROM (Optical Disc Read-Only Memory) and **Optical Memory Cards** are two other members of the ROM-Digital household. Both store large volumes of digital machine-readable data (1 to 4 MB on an OROM; 2 to 6 MB on cards).

OROM is comprised of concentric tracks (not the one continuous track of the CD discs). The concentric tracks, which match the tracking scheme of most magnetic media, allow faster access to data (than CD-ROMs) and for discs to rotate at Constant Angular Velocity (CAV). OROMs have been produced in 13 cm (5¼ inch) discs.

In summary, members of the ROM (Read-Only Memory) family all provide a means to distribute specialized and large amounts of data. In each case, the data—once produced on the discs—cannot be erased or updated. Moreover, the replication process (via stamping or injection molding) offers the information provider an economical, compact, durable way to get machine-readable data to a wide number of information users. These characteristics have lead to dubbing some Optical Read-Only-Memory media as 'Optical Publishing' systems. The other two Optical Memory families address quite different information-related needs.

THE WRITE-ONCE FAMILY

The Write-Once family of optical media can store data directly. Data is enscribed—by the creation of bubbles to represent pits and lands—onto Write-Once media by a laser beam. The laser is more high-powered than the laser beam used to read (only) data on ROM media. Once data is written onto Write-Once media it cannot be erased. Thus, Write-Once media is ideal for creating a permanent (10 years or so) record or audit trial. The Write-Once family has been subjected to several acryomyns, including WORM (Write-Once-Read-Many), OD3 or OD-Cubed (Optical Digital Data Disc). The reader (and various authors) will no doubt have a favorite. One acronym in this family is noteworthy, namely DRAW. DRAW (Direct Read After Write) refers to a writing method which immediately verifies the accuracy of each data block as it is written onto the disc (versus waiting until all data has been written). This technique is used on some, but not all, Write-Once media.

Unlike ROM data which can be mass-replicated onto ROM media, Write-Once media requires the laser beam to write directly onto each storage unit. Even with high data transfer rates, producing multiple copies would be slow (similar to copying data from 10 Winchester disks to 10 other Winchester disks). Thus, Write-Once media is viewed primarily as a means to archive data or store large amounts of data compactly online. Additionally, Write-Once media can be used to form custom or on-demand anthologies of data from an information provider's (or publisher's) database.

THE CD 'TRIPLETS'

The Compact Disc brothers (of the ROM-Digital Household) can be considered triplets. Like triplets, they have certain physical characteristics in common, yet each has its own 'personality' and 'mate'—its player/drive.

Each shares a common physical size (4.72 inches); each contains digital data; each has a tightly-bound spiral track (3-miles long if uncoiled); and the pits-and-lands pattern of each title is mass-produced.

Their 'personality' differences are summarized by their areas of expertise (i.e., for what tasks they are best suited) and the corresponding features of their 'spouses' or 'mates'—the drive on which they are played.

CD-Digital Audio is expert in storing sound—60 minutes of stereo. Its mate is a player whose function is to read the stored data, convert the digital signals into analog signals (sounds), and transfer the signals to speakers.

CD-Interactive is expert in storing audio, video, images and data (programs and/or text). Its expertise is in always storing each mode of information according to an agreed upon set of rules. Its mate, therefore, focuses on an established set of routines to bring out the contents of the CD-I disc. The mate has a built-in microprocessor and mechanisms to change the audio digital signals to sound, to change the video digital signals to video images, to change digital signals into page images, line art and graphics, and to change digital signals into ASCII text.

CD-ROM, the third triplet is the most versatile, free-form member of the trio. It can handle any type of digital data, including all the forms CD-I specializes in. Because it can handle any type of digital data and because it is such an undisciplined spirit, CD-ROM requires a 'smarter' mate that can also handle any form of data and figure out how CD-ROM has stored it away. In fact, the mate works with a separate microcomputer just to figure out CD-ROM and get the best performance from CD-ROM.

Sibling Rivalry

The CD-Digital Audio triplet and his mate are the most popular couple, welcomed in thousands of homes worldwide. CD-I, is still maturing, and his mate won't be available until sometime in 1987. But already the CD-Is are perceived as 'adorable'. When they are ready, they will also be welcomed in many homes and schools—especially where they can entertain and teach. In contrast, CD-ROM and his mate are more welcomed in businesses and wherever specialized or large information needs exist. The CD-ROMs play best with librarians, information specialists, and other people involved in a wide variety of information-based technical and business activities.

Theoretically, write-once discs could be used as a form of optical publishing, if the data were placed on the media along with the tracks at the initial manufacturing of the discs. Then multiple copies, presumably with space reserved for write-once storage by the user, could be quickly produced. It should be kept in mind that Write-Once media requires the use of a variable intensity laser beam to write data (higher-power laser needed) and to read data.

TRACKS BEFORE AND AFTER WRITING

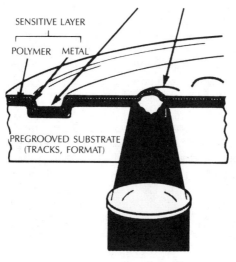

SENSITIVE LAYER

POLYMER   METAL

PREGROOVED SUBSTRATE
(TRACKS, FORMAT)

FIGURE 8:

Write-Once Recording

In a write-once system, a high-power laser etches digital bits onto the sensitive middle layer which has been preformatted with tracks. The outer layers (of plastics or glass) protect the disc from environmental elements (like dirt, dust) that otherwise might harm or alter the stored data. Many types of Write-Once discs are also packaged in protective cartridges.

The Write-Once Analog Household

Currently, the only application for writing analog data onto an optical media is in the creation of a videodisc. If the Write-Once version of the videodisc functions according to design, the producers usually create multiple copies of the videodisc using ROM manufacturing techniques.

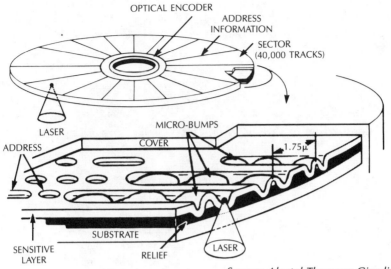

Source: Alcatel Thomson Gigadisc

FIGURE 9:

Write-Once Discs

Once information is written to Write-Once discs, the laser beam (at low intensity) is used to read data. Stored information is randomly accessible by locating the sector, according to its address. For very large database environments, jukebox-type mechanisms are available to automate the loading and changing Write-Once discs within the write/read drive.

The Write-Once Digital Household

Members of the Write-Once Digital household are generally seen as long-awaited solutions to records management, transaction logging, and archival of business data. In an environment where an estimated 76 million letters and 234 million photocopies are created daily in the United States alone, and where 90% of business information is kept on paper (Business Communications Company, Stamford, CT, private study, Sept. 1986), the prospect of optical storage is very appealing. Large amounts of business information, transactions and records can be stored digitally on Write-Once media. In addition to text (in ASCII representation), digital bit maps of images and paper transactions can be stored.

Write-Once Discs come in various sizes, including 14", 12", 8" and 5¼" diameter sizes. Due to variations in size, data formats, and writing techniques, the developers of each media are also developers (or in partnership with developers) of the unique disc recorder/drive for each media variation.

To allow for recording directly on the media, the storage density of write-once discs is less than that of ROM discs, but greater than the storage density of magnetic media. Figure 10 is a chart listing the storage capacity of several write-once discs.

FIGURE 10:

Comparison of Various Write-Once Media Storage Capacity

COMPANY	DISC DIAMETER	CAPACITY
STC	12″	4.0 Gigabytes
Hitachi	12″	1.3 Gigabytes
Toshiba	12″	1.2 Gigabytes
Sanyo	12″	18,000 page images
NEC	12″	15,000 page images or 1.3 Gigabytes
Mitsubishi	12″	37,400 frames
OSI	12″	1.0 Gigabytes
Optimem	12″	1.0 Gigabytes
Thomson CSF	12″	1.0 Gigabytes
Matsushita	8″	0.7 Gigabytes
FOA	12″	0.6 Gigabytes
Sony	8″	9,000 page images

CD-PROM is, unfortunately, a poor acronym for a write-once disc which matches the CD-ROM dimensions (4.72″) and spiral tracking pattern. The 'CD-PROM' (which stands for Compact Disc-Programmable Read-Only Memory) label is unfortunate since 'PROM' already is used to accurately describe a type of integrated circuit card. Furthermore, the term is misleading in the context of optical memory since the 'P' does not refer exclusively to a set of program instructions nor does a CD-PROM share the 'rewrite' capacity of a PROM chip. CD-PROM, like other write-once discs, requires a higher-powered laser beam for recording data. Once data is written, the disc could be read by ROM-digital drives (provided the CD-PROM conforms to standards for that CD-ROM system). CD-PROMs are still in experimental stages.

Write-Once Cards (also known as Optical Memory Cards and Laser-Card™) first received nationwide attention when Blue Cross/Blue Shield of Maryland announced its LifeCard™—a write-once card, about the size of a credit card on which a person's medical history, current prescriptions, X-rays, and other pertinent medical information could be stored. By carrying this card, the insured, even during a medical emergency, could provide critical medical data. Upon receipt of medical care and prescriptions, new data would be added to the write-once card. LaserCards™ are available in custom sizes and formats through Drexler Technologies. Up to 2 million bytes of data (about 800 pages of text) can be stored on a card. Thus far, those using or planning to use LaserCards™ include banks (for transaction logging and account status), government and business (for identification/ entry controls and for automotive/equipment maintenance records, etc.) medical institutions, and schools (for transcripts, test results). In each case, due to the custom design of the card, write-once card readers/writers are built to match the application.

To summarize, the Write-Once family of optical storage offers alternative or complementary solutions to microforms and online files for archiving, logging and managing transactions and records. Almost 3,000 installations exist. Users of Write-Once optical media are large organizations like American Express, NASA, insurance companies, government—all who have extensive archival and records managment needs.

THE ERASABLE FAMILY

While information providers are most enthused about ROM optical storage and records managers and administrators are most enthused about the potential for Write-Once optical storage, computer scientists, EDP and MIS professionals are focusing on erasable optical storage. Erasable optical storage, like magnetic storage, allows the user to store data and write over stored data when the previously-stored data is no longer needed.

The appeal of erasable optical storage is multi-level. Erasable optical storage (sometimes referred to as magneto-optical or MO), like other optical storage media, is a plastic-encased disc with tracks. Data is written via a high-powered laser beam which creates blisters or bubbles in the metallic layer of the disc. To change data, the laser heats the surface of the blister to alter it or to apply a magnetic charge. Blisters, less than a micromillimeter in size, permit high-density storage of data. The discs are less expensive to produce than aluminum-based Winchesters and hold up to ten times the data of Winchester disks. Compared to the shelf life of data on magnetic disks (12 to 18 months) and magnetic tape (36 months), optical discs have an estimated shelf life of 10 years and are not sensitive to heat, dust, etc.

As personal and departmental computer users generate more data to maintain electronically, companies are facing a growing demand for online storage. Increasing requirements for mass storage—especially in conjunction with digital image capture and handling—exist in companies of all sizes. Common problems include:

- Databases too large to maintain online, causing system management and access problems when data needs to be updated or reviewed.
- Image files too large for magnetic storage (and not easily broken into smaller components), forcing manual handling of graphic information.
- Expense of maintaining mass storage online.

- Offline storage of large amounts of data, restricting data access and creating additional layers of data management tasks.
- Mass storage on magnetic media (tape and disks), requiring periodic rewriting to maintain data.

While the need (and interest) in erasable optical storage is understandably high, viable products to function as computer peripherals for mass online storage are at least another two years away. Changing the value of a 'bubble' (versus the process used to create permanent marks created on Write-Once media) with a laser has proved difficult. Hence, no standard media sizes, etc., exist. Yet another (unfortunate) acronym is already in use for the future family member which will store digital data and match the 12 cm (4.72") diameter plastic disc: **CD-EPROM** (for Compact Disc-Erasable Programmable Read-Only Memory).

SECTION SUMMARY

Each household of optical storage addresses specific mass storage needs:
- The Erasable family is the next generation of storage media for data processing applications.
- The Write-Once family will complement and in some cases replace media now used for archiving data, namely paper file cabinets, microfilm.
- The ROM family offers the ability to distribute large volumes of information (text, graphics, video, and/or sound) in low-cost, compact form.

Given the number of optical storage media with the 'CD' prefix and the recent number of articles about optical storage media, this genealogy will help keep variations of optical storage media in perspective. With the rapidly changing nature and developments in optical memory technology, the reader may find it helpful to continue to categorize optical storage media:
— First by whether it is Read-Only, Write-Once, or Erasable
— Second by whether it stores data in digital or analog form
— Third by its physical dimensions and characteristics
— Finally by its current/intended use or application.

The market for optical storage is expected to expand rapidly as products and their standards become available. For all variations of optical storage of digital data, the world market in 1985 was about $200-million. Optical storage of digital data in 1990 is estimated to be a $8.5-billion market (according to Electronic Trend Publications's report entitled "Optical Memory's Impact on Magnetic Storage and Computer Systems Architecture", August, 1986). Other published reports likewise suggest (or hope for) a rapid adoption of the technology.

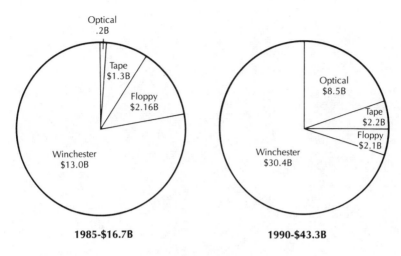

Mass Storage Market [$Billions]

FIGURE 11:

The Anticipated Influence of Optical Storage Media

A report from Electronic Trends Publications (Cupertino CA, August 1986) esti-mates the impact of all forms of optical storage on computer mass storage, office automation and publishing.

Further evidence of a promising future for optical storage media and systems is the involvement of over 130 companies researching and offering optical storage products. Many of these are major companies—3M, Sony, Phillips, Hitachi, Matsushita, Digital Equipment Corporation, Atari, Ver-batim, etc. A bright future also is suggested by the progress made in developing standards for certain optical media and their players, and the high levels of interest by publishers (both print-based and online), com-puter and peripheral suppliers, and information users in better storage and delivery systems.

CD-ROM SYSTEMS AND APPLICATIONS

While all optical storage media offer exciting possibilities for different kinds of information storage and retrieval situations, CD-ROM is especially interesting both to publishers and to those providing publishing services. Before we explore what's involved in creating a CD-ROM-based publication, let's first look at how CD-ROMs are used to distribute large amounts of data and for what types of applications CD-ROMs have been produced.

CD-ROM SYSTEMS

To read and use data contained on a CD-ROM requires:

- a CD-ROM player, containing a drive and software to accurately read data.
- a cable or connecting link to a computer so data read from the CD-ROM can be transferred to a computer.
- a computer with a monitor to receive and display data read from the disc.
- software to properly locate and interpret data into a form the user needs.

Optionally, a CD-ROM system may also have stereo speakers, a color monitor, laser printer and other perpherials.

CD-ROM drives are available from Sony, Philips, Digital Equipment Corporation (Philips-manufactured), Hitachi, and Denon America, and Reference Technologies (a customized Hitachi). Two such drives are shown in Figures 13 and 14.

Most manufacturers of CD-ROM drives do not offer complete systems. Instead, companies who function as system integrators (like DEC) or CD-ROM producers (like Reference Technologies) combine individual components and software for a given application. (A list of companies offering these services is available in Section 5). Thus, at this stage of CD-ROM development, a user of a CD-ROM system most likely has purchased or leased a CD-ROM system based on a particular application or CD-ROM product. Thanks to standards[3] for physical size, tracking format and data blocks, any of the CD-ROM drives could, theoretically, be used. Integra-

---

[3] A discussion of CD-ROM standards appears in Section 4.

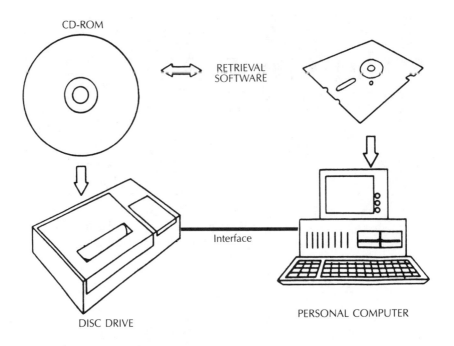

FIGURE 12:

Components of an Integrated CD-ROM System

FIGURE 13:

**This top-loading CD-ROM drive is offered on an OEM basis
from North American Philips.**

FIGURE 14:

Front-loading CD-ROM drives, such as this one from Sony, are also available.

tors will select one drive over others based on its overall fit within the integrated system, performance, cost, availability, etc. But, as with drive components within personal computers, once a drive is selected, software and hardware development will usually incorporate characteristics of that drive to achieve optimum system performance.

The drives themselves range in price from $1,200 to $2,000. This is considerably more than the cost of a consumer CD-Audio player (some models are about $150) due to the required mechanisms and software necessary for accurate reading of each digital data block.

The defacto standard computer used in the majority of integrated CD-ROM systems today is an IBM PC or compatible. In the library market, for example, almost all are based on the IBM-PC. Other computers, such as the Apple Macintosh or MicroVAX, could also be configured as part of a CD-ROM system. When the application for the CD-ROM system is highly specialized or used within a closed environment, customized systems pose no problem. However, if the CD-ROM system is to be used with several CD-ROMs from multiple publishers for a variety of applications and in differing environments, a more standard configuration is obviously desirable.

CD-ROM APPLICATIONS

This section describes three major catagories of CD-ROM applications. We'll begin with the most commonly available application, the use of CD-ROM database to substitute or complement the online version of the database. Next, we will look at the creation of reference materials and new databases, based on other media. Thirdly, we will explore CD-ROM applications designed to eliminate paper-based distribution of selected kinds of information.

CD-ROM VERSIONS OF ONLINE DATABASES

Many existing CD-ROM products are portable, fixed-priced versions of existing online databases. Information is essentially the same as the corresponding online version, with, perhaps periodic replacement CD-ROMs to reflect changes or updates to the data. Major benefits of a CD-ROM version of an electronic database are:

1. Fixed cost (instead of variable cost) for the information seeker. Databases on CD-ROM are available for a one-time or annual cost. A set price for a large volume of data must be weighed against the online costs, telecommunications costs, and often, subscription/membership charges incurred when querying online databases for the same data. Online connect time, particularly during prime times and for selected databases, can quickly translate to hundreds of dollars. Charges further escalate if the information seeker is not skilled in how to quickly pinpoint information electronically.

2. Lower distribution costs for the information provider. The cost of sending a CD-ROM in the mail ($0.22-$0.39 First Class) is substantially less than mailing hard copies or transmitting data to the information seeker.

3. More flexibility in searching alternatives. Especially when the CD-ROM contains searching software which is appropriate, helpful or established for the content of the CD-ROM database, the information seeker is not forced to use searching routines which are inefficient or cumbersome for the application.

4. No restrictions on when the information seeker can access data. The information seeker does not have to fit database use into times dictated by online availability or time-sensitive rates.

5. Data already stored locally. Data, once located, does not have to be transferred to magnetic media for subsequent (offline) perusal.

6. Possible addition of graphic data to supplement text.

A variety of CD-ROM versions of online databases exists. The majority are bibliographic in nature. Usually, these bibliographic CD-ROMs are, like their online counterparts, devoted to a particular subject or science. About 75 titles have been produced or are now in process. For example, CD-ROM titles are available on each of the following subjects:

Chemistry (abstracts of journals, conference proceedings and research reports from Chemical Abstract Society's database; from William Fraser a chemicals directory; and from the Royal Society of Chemistry international abstracts for all levels of chemists entitled Biotechnology Abstracts)

Education (the database listing of educational materials from NICEM,

the National Information Center for Education Media and the wi‹
referenced Educational Resources Information Center E
bibliography)

Engineering (abstracts of published articles, technical reports
conference proceedings)

Finance and Business (listings of SEC filings and stock registrati
Dun and Bradstreet financial and business data from its or
database for its business customers; and selected data containe
one CD-ROM from four existing financial databases of Disclo;
Predicasts, Media General, and Business Research Corporation]

Government research, developments and funding (abstracts
National Technical Information Society)

Law records and cases (bibliography of Library of Congress's
records, Eurolex's listings of European case law)

Medicine and Health (Excerpta Medica's abstracts, psyco
abstracts)

Scientific (the 110,000 abstracts of Aquatic Sciences and Fish‹
Abstracts from Cambridge Scientific Abstracts)

Library/Information Science (numerous bibliographies used b
brarians, professional information scientists and the public to lc
printed and audiovisual materials, including Library & Informa
Science Abstracts (LISA), the 1.4 million MARC records of all Lit
of Congress cataloging since 1964, and the MARVLS list of all Lit
of Congress holdings).

Full-text databases allow the user to seek and obtain desired infor
from the database itself. In comparison, bibliographical databases h
information seeker determine from the abstract or keyword labels
in the full text of the document. The majority of existing online dat
are bibliographic. Hence the majority of CD-ROM databases create
online databases are also bibliographic. However, a few full-text CL
databases have been produced from online, full-text electronic data
Examples of full-text CD-ROM databases (from existing online data
are:

POISINDEX (containing the ingredients of various substances, m‹
facturer data and toxiological data/treatment)

DRUGEX (data about both approved and experimental drugs)

INDENTIDEX (containing the drug manufacturer's imprint co‹
and description for tablets and capsules identification)

EMERGINDEX (with relevant medical data regarding diagnosis
treatment of various medical conditions)

The **Corporate Information Database** (with information on the
formance, industry ranking, strategies, personnel, research activit
etc. of more than 10,000 firms in the United States) as well as o
financial/business databases.

Comparing CD-ROM Versions with Online Database Versions

The appropriateness of a CD-ROM version of a database to its online counterpart is determined by 3 basic factors:

a) frequency of change in database content
b) additional features in the CD-ROM version to increase the value or improve the use of data
c) cost differential.

Rate of Data Change

Certain types of data don't change over time. For example, a legal case history, itself, doesn't change. However, additional, related data could be desired. Subsequent interpretations of the case, regulatory or legal changes, and uses of the case history may be useful to the information seeker. Such changes could occur at any time. Likewise, some medical data remains relatively constant over time. Other medical information changes with new findings or procedures.

If the data is on CD-ROM, changes cannot be made directly to the disc. However, as in printed materials, periodic updates (or revisions) can be made. A newly–updated complete database on CD-ROM could be created and distributed, replacing the previous versions. In a practical sense (due to manufacturing cycles), updates could be new CD-ROMs on a monthly, quarterly, semi–annually, annually or occasional basis.

In other cases, the data content is too volitale for distribution on CD-ROM. Often, in these cases, the primary value of online databases is the ability to almost immediately reflect the most current information amid more static data. Current stock values, this week's Nielsen ratings, daily and weekly news summaries are examples of constantly changing data whose value is directly linked to its currency. Databases whose material must be updated weekly or more often than weekly are usually not good candidates for CD-ROM.

Added Features/Value

Besides database contents, some CD-ROM titles or systems also have special features to simplify use or to extend the information seeker's use of the data. These features may be data structure/capability, software programs or system configurations.

A good example of enhancements for the user are found with Datek's CD-ROM of corporate data. Along with financial/business database (the Corporate Information Database), disc-resident software provides the user with menus for easier data access. In addition, data is directly compatible with some popular PC-based spreadsheet programs. This allows the user to directly incorporate data into tables, reports, etc.

Many examples of value-added CD-ROM databases can be found in library applications. As leaders in the use of online services and databases

for various library functions, libraries are also focal points for CD-ROM products. CD-ROM bibliographic databases are used not only for identifying pertinent articles and materials. They are also a means (or part of a system) for ordering or acquiring materials, creating catalog cards and union lists, and controlling circulation. Thus, in some cases, the CD-ROM version supplements an online system, rather than competing with an online database. The description of a few library-oriented CD-ROMs will illustrate their value-added features.

The Library Corporation, creator of the first CD-ROM title, publishes monthly complete catalog records of the Library of Congress. The user can search the database by ISSN, ISBN, Library of Congress card number, author, title, type of work, when published, etc. Menus are provided to help the user search. Once the desired MARC record is located, the user has a number of options, including the creation of a printed library catalog card (in the format of the library), the creation of spine or pocket labels, checking to see if the desired item is currently checked out (if a circulation program is used in conjunction with the system), locating other libraries with the item, and copying the catalog information to an acquisition request form. Thus, several tasks can be accomplished quickly and easily through a combination of the database with supporting and integrated hardware and software.

Another aspect of library automation is addressed through Ingram Book Company's LaserSearch system. The system, consisting of an IBM PC (XT or AT), monitor, Hitchi CD-ROM drive, and modem, uses a CD-ROM of all books in Ingram's inventory. Software not only allows the user to locate desired publications, it helps the user create book orders, submit a group of orders electronically to Ingram, and maintain records of book orders and acquisition funding.

Another CD-ROM product delivering more than database information is offered by Faxon. Its MicroLink system (with an IBM PC and Hitachi CD-ROM drive) is a serials control system, to monitor and control periodical circulation, purchases, and inventory. The CD-ROM, containing the Library of Congress MARC-S serials catalog and updated quarterly, is used in the creation of the library's own serials catalog records and files.

Thus, the value-added nature of the CD-ROM may be addition software—especially to help with or replace difficult searching algorithms—and/or data compatibility so information can be directly used with other programs or with other system components.

Cost—Often the Ultimate Factor between the Online or CD-ROM Version

Online databases charge for information access on a usage basis plus subscription fee (one-time sign-up and/or continuing). In addition, the user has to pay for telecommunications (connect) time. Charges also vary according to the information provider's fee (ranging from $25.00 to

$350.00 per hour) and telephone rates at different times of day. Other factors in the cost of using online databases are a) the sophistication of database structure and b) the user's ability to efficiently create clever search arguments for quick, accurate pinpointing of data. Thus, the user never knows for certain how much the online charges will be.

In comparison, the CD-ROM version is sold at a fixed price. The price for a given CD-ROM depends on the value the information seller puts on the database. Frequently, the CD-ROM price will be for the initial database and some number of replacement discs over the course of one year. Pricing of selected CD-ROMs, presented in Figure 15, gives a representative view of current costs.

FIGURE 15:

Representative costs to user for CD-ROM distribution of information.

	CD-ROM Price	Approximate Cost of CD Components to Add to User's PC
Full-text Reference (Grolier's encyclopedia)	$199	Included in CD-ROM price
Bibliographic Database (LC MARC)	$870 for 4 discs (quarterly update) $1,470 for 12 discs (monthly update)	$3,000
Financial Database (Datek's Corporate Index)	$10,000 for 36 discs (monthly update) (A 4-disc set for each edition)	$2,500

If a database is used on rare occasions, or infrequently, the online version will probably be more cost-effective. However, for frequently-used databases or for complex or lengthy searches within a database, a CD-ROM version is usually less expensive. Moreover, the CD-ROM version is usually less stressful as well, since the user doesn't feel 'the meter running' as with online services.

SPECIALIZED AND GENERAL REFERENCE MATERIALS FROM OTHER MEDIA

The next category of CD-ROM applications are specialized materials or reference databases from other media. Unlike the previous category (where the content of online databases are distributed on CD-ROM), this group of applications includes more customized packaging of data, the inclusion of images as well as text, and in some cases, the use of specialized, single-application systems.

Several information providers and publishers have been studying CD-ROMs for the creation of general reference materials. Only one general reference product for use in the home or office is currently for sale: Grolier's *Academic American Encyclopedia*. The disc contains the text of an entire encyclopedia set. The user can browse through the text, access a specific topic through keyword or full-text searches, and quickly jump to cross-referenced portions of the encyclopedia. The Grolier disc was based on an online version of the encyclopedia, which included data structures for searching and cross-referencing. Therefore, no graphic images (e.g. maps, diagrams, photos) nor digital audio or video were included. This CD-ROM encyclopedia sells for $199 and does not require the usual amount of shelf space one must normally reserve for a 25-volume set of books. What is required is a personal computer and a CD-ROM drive. Future general reference CD-ROMs will, no doubt, include digital images, sound, etc. as appropriate, especially after the sample/prototype *MultiMedia Encyclopedia*[4] illustrated the power of combining audio-visual aids with textual data. Other general reference materials under consideration for home use include telephone directories, service manuals and product catalogs.

Customer-specific CD-ROM databases are available. A publisher or information provider can package onto a CD-ROM collections of information, anthologies of journals, or previously-published data suited for a particular market or interest group. One example is the way Datatek has expanded its newspaper clipping service, by offering newspapers customized CD-ROM databases. Instead of large amounts of space for paper archives or microfilm archives (which is not easily indexed or referenced and is usually backlogged in production), the newspaper's 'morgue' can be on CD-ROMs. An added bonus in this application (over paper or microform archives) is the ability to reuse the previously-published information (for publication or notetaking) without having to reenter the data. Since the cost per disc (Datatek charges $200 per disc for a minimum of 50 discs or $30 per disc for more than 1,000 copies of the disc.) decreases with larger quantities of CD-ROMs, newspapers may also want to sell their 'morgue' to other publishers and information outlets to defray CD-ROM production costs. According to Datatek, about a dozen newspapers have installed the necessary MicroVAX computer, CD-ROM drive and searching software.

CD-ROM databases have also been created as alternatives to reference databases which were previously stored in microform. Brodart offers a CD-ROM version of its COM (Computer Output Microfilm) library catalog of over 1 million listings. Known as *LePac*, the disc version, is intended for library patron use. The cost of the CD-ROM version is about the same as

---

[4] The *MultiMedia Encyclopedia* is described in more detail later in this section.

the microfilm version, but patrons should find the CD-ROM version easier to use and faster in accessing the desired citation. The system (using special terminals with simplified pads and an Hitachi CD-ROM drive) is being tested within the Los Angeles County system.

Other microfilm replacements include University Microfilm Institute's CD-ROM which combines facsmile images of *IEEE Journal* pages with a machine-readable (ASCII) index; and Information Handling Services' index of military specifications and military standards (known as TechData). Previously on microfilm, the CD-ROM version of TechData involves the conversion of more than 65,000 vendor catalogs and will allow the user to perform full-text searches on the index. The TechData disc will be updated monthly and is expected to cost between $5,000 and $6,000 for an annual subscription.

The first planned CD-ROM version of a digital videodisc is from National Decision Systems. The disc contains statistical, demographic and geographic data and marketing information on consumer and retail expenditures. As with its larger brother (the digital videodisc), the CD-ROM version of the Infomark PC-based system will allow the user to overlay data onto color maps of the entire United States or any geographic portion of the country.

Another CD-ROM illustrates how a CD-ROM database a) has been created from previous media, b) is customized for a particular use/user, and c) sometimes requires a customized system. "The Universe of Sound, Volume One" from Optical Media Services is a CD-ROM for use in the recording and broadcast industry. It contains a large number of files of digital music data which had been previously stored on floppy diskettes. Several hundred sound effects, sounds of individual musical instruments, combined sounds of different instruments, etc. are stored. Unlike sounds stored on CD-Audio, these sounds are stored for use only within an online digital emulator. The emulator is used to professionally mix sound for television/film music, recordings, etc. The system hardware consists of an Apple Macintosh, a Sony CD-ROM drive, special interfaces and the sound mixing, emulation device (called Emulator II). Files are accessed via commands at the Macintosh. As a digital sound file is read by Sony CD-ROM drive, the digital data is transferred directly into the Emulator II keyboard. The advantages of CD-ROM storage in this application are the increased storage capacity compared to floppy diskette and a 60% reduction in response time (for accessing and transferring the digital sound file to the emulator).

And, finally, although this reference database exists only as a demonstration product, the *MultiMedia Encyclopedia* illustrates how effective and exciting a reference database on CD-ROM can be. Compiled from printed material, recordings, and pictures, the MME contains the text as well as audio of historic speeches; stills of actual events set to music; symphonies heard while reading about the symphony and seeing sheet music; color images which can be enlarged for closer analysis; motion sequences of migratory paths, animal and chemical behavior; multiple language explanations of the same visual image; annotated text, etc. By using sound and color images, the MME demonstrates the value of hearing (as well as reading) and the richness images and motion sequences can lend to understanding.

PAPERLESS DISTRIBUTION

In the quest for better control and access to paper-based information, several innovative CD-ROMs have been created. In most cases, the information provider views the disc as a compact way to distribute data, even if hard copy (paper) versions of the data are generated for user reference. Unlike the CD-ROM products previously discussed, which were generally created from nonprint databases, these CD-ROMs are addressing applications where the majority of data was largely paper-based. As such, the incorporation of graphic images (frequently found in printed materials) was often required.

The advantages of each of the discs described in this section are:
- lower distribution cost
- reduced filing/bookshelf space requirements
- no wear or deterioration of information materials
- completeness of files (pages or parts of the database can't be misplaced, etc.)
- faster access to desired data
- potential reuse of data (without rekeyboarding to put in machine-readable form).

Collections of Technical Designs and Specifications

Three different CD-ROMs were created for better distribution and access to technical diagrams and component specifications. One, the Tech-Doc/Digital Database from Inacom International, contains fact sheets and diagrams of circuit boards. Engineers can both 'browse' through the database and/or electronically search for specific characteristics about semiconductors and integrated circuit boards.

A special engineering design system with a CD-ROM drive is under development so engineers can then take the data directly from disc for use in design tasks.

Another CD-ROM, from a distributor of engineering system components (Xebec), is a product catalog containing product characteristics, specifications, pricing, and product assembly instructions. The disc is intended for both internal personnel and customers. Digital Equipment Corporation also plans to distribute product specifications and documentation on CD-ROMs. Each CD-ROM requires diagrams and illustrations to fully describe products, assembly components, etc.

Another technical catalog system, developed for a manufacturer, allows the service representative to access the part number while viewing a labelled schematic of a device (or portion of machinery). The user can, at the same time, create an order form to take the required items from inventory and also create an itemized parts bill for the customer.

Instruction and Service Manuals

Large amounts of instruction materials—to supplement coursework, to provide self-paced courses, and/or to serve as ongoing reference—can be contained on a CD-ROM. One such disc is planned by Academic Micro-broadcasting Educational Network as a companion to its television course-ware. Contents will be suitable for coursework on a system and for generating coursework in hardcopy.

A number of computer manufacturers and software suppliers are, reportedly, considering publishing instructional and service manuals on CD-ROM. Discs could include the software programs as well as instructions on their use.

Regulations and Other References

Currently the state code of the Commonwealth of Virginia is available on CD-ROM. In addition to allowing law firms to locate revelant regulations, full-text passages can be 'lifted' and incorporated in briefs and other legal documentation.

CD-ROMS containing other regulations, including the IRS Code and other federal government statutes, serve yet other professions in a similar fashion.

Forms

Another technique for paperless distribution is the creation of 'form discs'. On the CD-ROM are forms, standard letters and documents which can be printed on demand, as needed, cutting down on inventories of preprinted materials. Additionally, the user has the option to modify a 'form letter', for example, by first calling the (reusable) text onto an editing screen prior to printing.

Since even the federal government would have a difficult time filling the contents of a CD-ROM with forms, the forms accompany related data, such as IRS regulations or state statutes.

Maps, Charts and Navigational Systems

CD-ROMs containing digital maps and other geographical information are under development.

The GeoDisc from GeoVision is a collection of maps, geographic data and graphics. In conjunction with the GeoDesk system (an IBM PC-XT, high-resolution color monitor, CD-ROM drive, color graphics printer and special applications software), the user can call color maps to the screen, add data, boundaries, different colors, etc. The completed graphic image can be stored (on the PC's magnetic disk) and output on the color printer. The system reduces the time to generate customized maps and graphic data.

U.S. Geological Survey (USGS) is developing a CD-ROM for distributing LANDSAT images and other geological information.

One map storage disc from Geographic Data Technology would contain digitized street maps, including location of each house number, each intersection and the identification of expressways, one-way streets and limited-access streets. As with any map, multiple uses and applications are possible, such as commerical and leisure trip routing, creating carrier routes and zones, establishing sales territories, dispatching and sequencing personnel for deliveries and service calls. The system requires a personal computer along with the disc drive.

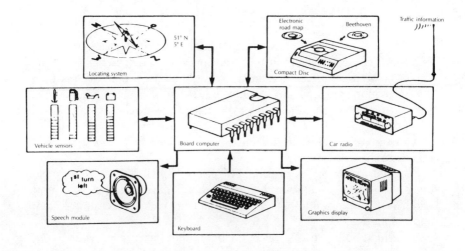

FIGURE 16:

The Philips CARIN™ system illustrates a custom CD-ROM integrated system for a special, navigational application.

A more specialized system is needed for the CD-ROM navigational system being developed by N.V. Philips. (See diagram, Figure 16). The system has been designed to help the driver find the best route, and advise the driver of the best alternate route based on efficient fuel consumption and current conditions (such as a traffic jam, bad weather, a wrong turn, etc.). The in-car systems works together with an orbiting space satellite which exchanges conditional data with the in-car computer and monitors the car's location. Options are even available to link sensors to the car or bus to advise the driver of low fuel, excess speed, etc. Obviously, the CD-ROM functions as just one peripheral in this customized system which is intended to be positioned within the dashboard. The disc stores digitized maps (for displaying images on the system's graphics monitor) and digital sound for supplying the driver with audible directions. The system, entitled CARIN™, is expected to go on sale in Europe in the later part of 1987. While such an elaborate system may not be necessary for running errands around one's hometown, such a system would be useful for taxis, truck drivers, travellers, etc. Similar, specialized navigational systems are already in use on military aircraft and ships.

SOFTWARE PUBLISHING

Although no CD-ROM products are exclusively devoted to distributing software, several software firms are considering CD-ROM for future distribution (versus floppy disks, magnetic tapes or rigid magnetic disks). Publishing software on CD-ROM avoids program piracy (where multiple copies of the program are created and distributed by someone other than the originating company and its agents). Another advantage of publishing software on CD-ROM is the ability to fit all the software on one disc (versus multiple floppies), including program variations for different computers and operating systems, documentation, tutorials, and even databases related to the software.

Imagine, for example, distribution on one, small disc of a complete digital font library, including graphic symbols (logos, etc.) plus all font width data, kerning tables, etc. to download into your composition system and output device.

Publishing software on CD-ROM offers the software provider more efficient, less expensive manufacturing and low distribution costs. Software publishers are, no doubt, anxiously waiting for more installed CD-ROM drives among their prospective customers before moving from magnetic media.

SUMMARY

As presented in this section, CD-ROM distribution of large volumes of data can supplement other forms of information distribution and access. In some cases, the CD-ROM version is a preferable alternative to other distribution methods. In yet other cases, the CD-ROM product offers unique benefits over any other media.

The number of CD-ROM titles and installed CD-ROM drives is still small. At this stage of adopting CD-ROM technology, many of the installed CD-ROM drives are configured with system hardware and software for a specific application or disc. In a customized system environment, the original disc provider and perhaps a few other companies active in that same vertical market/application will create additional CD-ROM titles for those users. However, for broader-based publishing of CD-ROM titles (similar to the proliferation of CD-Audio titles from a variety of recording companies), publishers will need to either create a demand for their CD-ROM driver/configuration or wait until an installed based of 'standard' systems exists. The long-anticipated announcement from IBM about a CD-ROM-based PC product, coupled with announced drives from Digital Equipment Corporation and Atari, suggest an increasing installed base in the near future.

Publishers, like Grolier, have experimented with CD-ROM, partly as an educational process. More publishers—especially those without experience in constructing electronic databases or capturing digital image—will be considering CD-ROM products. They, and those who provide them with print publishing services, need to learn more about what's involved in creating a CD-ROM.

PUBLISHING ON CD-ROM

The process of publishing—whether the final product is a printed book or a CD-ROM—involves numerous steps. Since the information published in print and on CD-ROM cannot be changed, special care is taken at each step to assure accuracy in the final product. Also, because the product is used by a number of people, often remote from the publisher, care is taken in designing the product, structuring and enhancing its content, and creating necessary reference components so the user can understand and use the information contained in the product.

In the print publishing world, product design would include the book format, page designs, the manner in which illustrations are used, typographic specifications, etc. Structuring and enhancing book contents would involve organizing and sequencing materials, deciding how many and what illustrations are required, editorial review, modifying copy to conform with standards of language and spelling, typesetting of copy, use of color, etc. Print reference components cover a range of elements, including folios (page numbers), running heads, footnotes, unique typographic variations for different text components, tables of contents, indexes, appendixes, and bibliographies.

A variety of specialists may be involved in these aspects of book publishing along with production specialists for platemaking, printing and binding. Likewise, many specialists are involved in CD-ROM.

In this section, we will first briefly describe how the use of a CD-ROM and the properties of a CD-ROM impact the publishing process. Then we will explain the process of publishing via CD-ROM. This section concludes with types of services available to help a publisher create a CD-ROM.

USING A CD-ROM PUBLICATION

Volume Implications

The enormous capacity of the CD-ROM (equal to a complete encyclopedia or about 150,000 pages) demands a way for the user to pinpoint the desired information quickly and easily. For many applications, the user will not browse serially through data. Instead, the user will want to see selected data at random. For some applications, the user may also want to maintain the ability to 'browse' or page through portions of the database as well. Good, flexible referencing, optimum structuring and clever design are essential.

Type of Content

Besides text and static images, a CD-ROM may contain motion sequences (video) and sound (audio). These additional communcation techniques not only add to dimensions to user understanding, they also add layers of design and production implications. For example, audio requires gaps between digital data for proper reading, thus taking up more disc space than digital text. Even brief motion sequences can quickly use up disc space, and digital images take significantly more digital storage than text. Since a CD-ROM has only a finite amount of space, its design must maximize a smooth transfer of information to the user while fitting all the required data, properly referenced on the disc (or multiple discs). To produce a CD-ROM with multiple types of digital data, special systems and expertise are necessary to convert all data to the proper format and mix the data appropriately for placement on the CD-ROM.

A Computer-based Delivery System

For a user to access data on a published CD-ROM, a computer-based system is required. A minimum CD-ROM delivery system involves hardware (a computer of some size, a monitor, a CD-ROM player and interface to the computer) plus software (both for searching/retrieving operations and for the application/user interface). Additional perpherials (e.g. speakers, color monitor and graphics circuit board, color printer) may be needed as well, depending on the CD-ROM content.

If a publisher decides to use an existing, already-established CD-ROM delivery system, the task of hardware integration can be avoided. If the publisher also chooses to use that delivery system's operating system and application programs, the task of software integration is avoided. Both

FIGURE 17:

Maximum storage capacity on CD-ROM for different types of data

Audio:	60-74 minutes of digital stereo music
	144 minutes of Hi-Fi quality stereo music
	10 hours of stereo speech (AM radio-quality)
Video:	5 to 6 minutes of motion video
Single images:	5,500 to 6,000 pictures (384 x 280 resolution)
	5,500 computer-generated images (256 colors)
	2,750 computer-generated images (32,768 colors)
	15,000 document pages (bit-mapped)
Text:	550-600 MB (about 150,000 pages)
Programs:	300 MB

hardware and software integration are specialized fields, usually foreign to the publisher's expertise. The tasks of developing and integrating hardware and/or software adds considerable time and expense to the publishing project.

In addition, the user would have additional cost beyond the price of the CD-ROM to acquire all or parts of the custom delivery system. However, the intended use of the CD-ROM (such as the vehicle navigation system described in the previous section) may require a specialized delivery system hardware and/or software. Normally, the type of delivery system hardware is determined by what installed systems exist in the target market for the CD-ROM.

More often, debate centers on software—whether to use existing software or develop custom software and whether to follow proposed standards defining various software aspects of a delivery system.[5] In the final analysis the suitability of delivery software and use of proposed software standards is based on the application and market for the planned CD-ROM product.

Decisions about the delivery system hardware and software can impact virtually every aspect of the CD-ROM publishing process. Therefore delivery system decisions should be made initially, prior to the production process. Subsequent development of hardware and/or software may be concurrent with portions of the publishing process.

The Screen 'Page'

Another implication of CD-ROM use is the way the user 'sees' the contents of a CD-ROM publication. Rather than seeing materials on a typeset printed page, contents are usually viewed on a screen. Screen resolution, limited display methods to differentiate elements, ways of formatting data for screen display, reference indicators, menus and prompts are new design factors.

Re-use of Data

A final implication of the CD-ROM use is the ability to reuse its contents. Since the information is already in machine-readable form, the user may wish to incorporate the data into a another document or spreadsheet and/or output selected data in hardcopy. Such subsequent, direct uses of the data mean the publisher must make provisions (in data structure and software) for compatibility with other software programs and system peripherals.

---

[5] Established standards—known as The Philips/Sony World Standard for CD-ROM—don't assure complete capability among all CD-ROM drives/players and CD-ROM disks, nor do they assure standardized formatting of data on each CD-ROM disk nor standardized files structures. More on standards in the final section.

CD-ROM PROPERTIES AND THEIR IMPLICATIONS FOR PUBLISHING

Besides the use/user implications in developing a CD-ROM product, a few properties of CD-ROM media are especially important to understand.

CD-ROM's Finite Elements

A CD-ROM's tiny, continuous spiral track is divided into sectors. Just as on floppy diskette, each sector has an 'address' so it can be randomly located by the drive mechanism. (For a better understanding of what is contained in a sector and how user data (bytes) are converted into the pits-and-lands pattern of channel bits see Figures 18 and 19).

A sector is the smallest addressable unit of a CD-ROM (just as the smallest addressable unit of a magnetic disks is a sector). Unlike magnetic disks where sector addresses are track # sector # (on disks with concentric tracks), or merely sector # (for disks with a spiral track), CD-ROM addresses are based on its sister's (CD-Audio) addressing conventions. Addresses are expressed in terms of 'playing time', divided into 60 minutes of playing time, 60 seconds with each minute, and 75 sectors within that

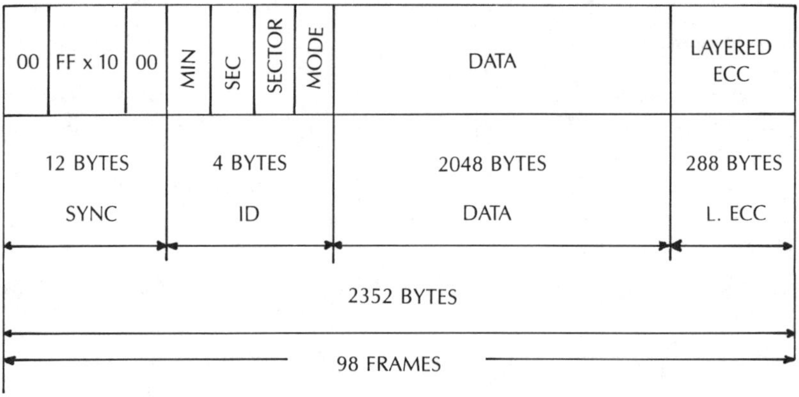

00	FF x 10	00	MIN	SEC	SECTOR	MODE	DATA	LAYERED ECC
12 BYTES			4 BYTES				2048 BYTES	288 BYTES
SYNC			ID				DATA	L. ECC

2352 BYTES

98 FRAMES

One CD ROM sector

FIGURE 18:

The Contents of One Sector on a CD-ROM

Each sector (or block) contains 2K (2,048 bytes) of user data, plus its address/identification (4 bytes), synchronizing data (12 bytes), and error correction data (288 bytes), for a total of 2,352 bytes per sector.

Bytes are grouped in frames (24 bytes to each frame). The frame is the basic information unit of CD-ROM writing and reading. There are 98 frames within each CD-ROM sector.

FIGURE 19:

Getting from user data (bytes) to the pits

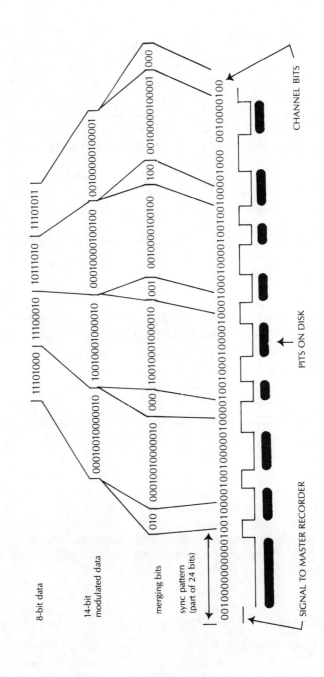

GETTING FROM USER DATA (BYTES) TO THE PITS

Each data byte (an 8 digit code or 8 'bits') is ultimately expressed in 'channel bits' of a pit-and-land pattern. Five basic steps are involved:

1. Each 8-bit (binary) code is converted to a 14-bit (binary) modulation code. This conversion, usually accomplished through a conversion look-up table, is to create the necessary run length of the data stream for proper reading by the CD-ROM drive.

2. Three additional merge bits are added to the 14-bit modulation code to clearly separate the beginning and end of each 14-bit symbol.

3. Each set of 24 bytes (each byte expressed as a 17-bit channel) is now a group known as a 'frame'—the basic data unit of CD-ROM.

4. To each frame, a synchronizing pattern (24 bits + 3 channel bits for proper 'separation'), a control & display code (14 bits + 3 bits), and error correction (8 x 17 channel bits) are added. The frame, consisting of 24 bytes (192 bits) of user data, has a total of 588 channel bits.

5. The frame's channel bits are the stream of 1s and 0s recorded as pits and lands. A 1 channel bit begins a pit. The pit continues to be etched for every 0 channel bit until another 1 channel bit is received. That 1 channel bit ends the pit and begins a land. The land continues as each 0 channel bit is read until another 1 channel pit ends the land and starts the next pit.

second. Thus, there are 270,000 (60 x 60 x 75) sectors on a CD. Each sector address includes its 'minute', 'second', and sector ('block'), represented as MM:SS:BB. For example, the 200th sector's address is expressed as 0:2:49 (zero minutes; 2 seconds; sector 49).

Fortunately, as with magnetic disks, the operating software of the delivery system (not the user) handles the accessing of sectors by the proper addressing conventions. However, understanding the sector arrangement is important for designing how data will be physically stored and sequenced on a CD-ROM.

Accessing Data on a CD-ROM

To access data from a revolving digital disc/disk (optical or magnetic) involves:

a) positioning the reading mechanism ('read-head') some distance along the radius of the disc so the proper track is under the read head (known as radial positioning)

b) stopping any movement of the read-head and focusing on the desired track (called 'settling')

c) once set, waiting as the disc revolves until the sector with the correct, desired address moves under the read-head ('latency')

d) reading the stored data

e) transferring the read data from the drive/reader.

The time for Steps a, b, and c are often referred to as 'seek time'. Obviously, depending on the distance the read-head has to move along the radius to get to the next sector and the sector location as the read-head is settling (e.g., just passing the read-head, about to pass, etc.) for any given seek, times fluctuate.

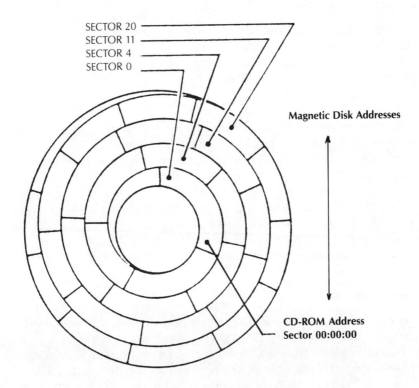

FIGURE 20:

Sector Addresses

Unlike magnetic disks where sector addresses are track #, sector # (on disks with concentric tracks), or merely sector # (for disks with a spiral track), CD-ROM addresses are based on its sister's (CD-Audio) addressing conventions. Each CD-ROM sector address includes its 'minute', 'second', and sector ('block'), represented as MM:SS:BB.

The price one pays for using the high-density storage capacity of CD-ROM (instead of magnetic disk storage) is in the time it takes to access data. The average access time for a CD-ROM is 3 seconds. This is several times slower than the average access times for magnetic media. For example, a Winchester (magnetic) disk is over 10 times faster in accessing data.[6]

Slow access times result in unacceptable lags in system performance. Any techniques to minimize access time and the number of seeks required to locate data are very important. Therefore, access time implications in a) designing the layout of the disc, b) determining the file structure, and c) creating efficient references, indexes, and directories within the application software must be considered.

CD-ROM Layout Options

To minimize access time, there are three basic ways to physically layout files on the CD-ROM:

1) Use contiguous, sequential sectors along the spiral track—contents of no other files or indexes are placed in those sectors

2) Map files, so file content is distributed in sectors located in various portions of the disc

3) Intermix files, breaking files into 2048-byte blocks (sectors) and alternate or interleaf with blocks or other divided files.

The best method to use will depend on the application and the nature of the database. For example, the interleaf technique works well in certain database applications because the index file—which must be referenced often and prior to accessing a portion of the database file—is in close physical proximity to the database file.

The goal of designing the geographic use of the CD-ROM is to reduce access times by keeping the distances between data as short as possible.

File Structures

Faster retrieval of data also depends on how files are structured. Physically, files are broken into 2,048 bytes (sectors) for storage on the CD-ROM and standards exist for a) the number of sectors on a CD-ROM, b) the contents of a sector—what coding conventions are used for synchronizing, error-checking and identifying the address and mode of the 2,048 bytes of file data, and c) what error-checking (Cross-Interleaved Reed-Solomon or CIRC) will be used. What doesn't yet exist are accepted standards on the logical aspects of file structure.

---

[6] The Winchester's radial positioning time is 40 to 70 milliseconds, compared to the CD-ROM's 500 milliseconds; its readhead settles over 612 tracks instead of 18,000 or so on the CD-ROM; and, by rotating at 3600 rpm (versus about 300 rpm for a CD-ROM), the Winchester's average latency time is only 8 milliseconds compared to CD-ROM's 60-150 milliseconds.

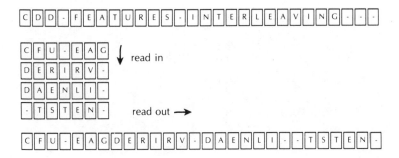

FIGURE 21:

The Intermix or Interleaf Technique

This is an example of data interleaving. Notice how this technique can concentrate data in one area instead of stringing data sequentially.

Source: Byte magazine, May 1986

Using a book as a model, a simple file structure would be: a table of contents, data files and an index structure. Many disk/disc operating systems for computers of all sizes use a similar structure. MS-DOS, for example, consists of a volume-directory-file structure. Yet to pinpoint data within a file, the application may require a file structure with more layers (e.g. volume-directory-subdirectory-file-subfile) or the ability to identify and locate files contained in different directories. While magnetic storage media can frequently circumvent file structuring restrictions through multiple seeks, limiting the number of seeks is more important in CD-ROM systems.

The publisher may opt to use a standard file structure or to develop a file structure that is particularly suited to the nature of the data and/or the CD-ROM application. If a custom file structure is used, special operating system software will be needed as well as application software.

With these various aspects of CD-ROM publishing described, we can now explore the steps in creating a CD-ROM.

PRODUCING A CD-ROM: THE PROCESS

There are at least 10 steps in producing a CD-ROM:
- Data capture
- Determining file structure
- Data enhancement
- Determining layout
- Indexing
- Testing
- Premastering

Full Text Search Is
Based on Words

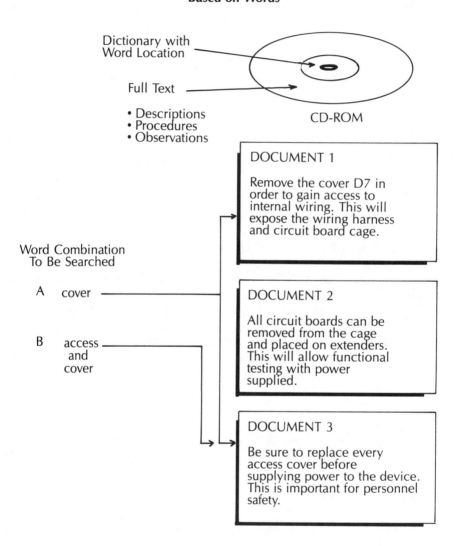

Dictionary with
Word Location

Full Text

• Descriptions
• Procedures
• Observations

CD-ROM

DOCUMENT 1

Remove the cover D7 in order to gain access to internal wiring. This will expose the wiring harness and circuit board cage.

Word Combination
To Be Searched

A   cover

B   access
      and
      cover

DOCUMENT 2

All circuit boards can be removed from the cage and placed on extenders. This will allow functional testing with power supplied.

DOCUMENT 3

Be sure to replace every access cover before supplying power to the device. This is important for personnel safety.

FIGURE 22, AND 23:

Searching and Retrieving Data

Full text searching requires a different system for locating data than searches of structured data files.

Source: Cunieform

Key Index Search Is
Based on Records

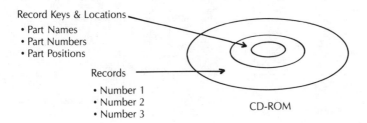

Record Keys & Locations
- Part Names
- Part Numbers
- Part Positions

Records

- Number 1
- Number 2
- Number 3

CD-ROM

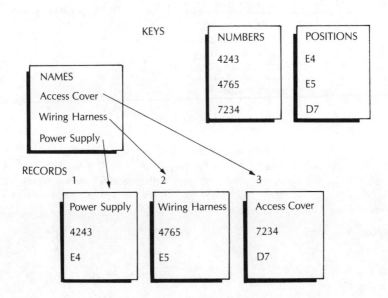

KEYS

NUMBERS	POSITIONS
4243	E4
4765	E5
7234	D7

NAMES
Access Cover
Wiring Harness
Power Supply

RECORDS
1　　　　2　　　　3

Power Supply	Wiring Harness	Access Cover
4243	4765	7234
E4	E5	D7

FIGURE 23

55

	1. Browse or Scan		Search Document	ENTER SEARCH WORDS:

1. Browse or Scan

2. Search by Topic

Search Document	ENTER SEARCH WORDS: Use _____ and _____
Display Text Sections	
Display Drawings	SECTIONS FOUND: 1. 2. 3.
Document Hardcopy	
Operating Instructions	DRAWINGS FOUND: 1.

Interactive Documentation

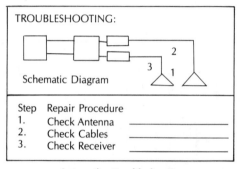

TROUBLESHOOTING:

Schematic Diagram

Step	Repair Procedure	
1.	Check Antenna	_____
2.	Check Cables	_____
3.	Check Receiver	_____

3. Diagnostic Search

4. Graphical Search

Interactive Troubleshooting

FIGURE 24:

Search and Retrieval Strategies

Different users and different information needs may require a single CD-ROM program to accommodate a variety of searching strategies. Software and file structures, in this example, must allow the user to organize and locate data differently, according to the situation.

Source: Cunieform

- Mastering
- Checking
- Manufacturing

In addition, a publisher may also be developing software and delivery systems for the CD-ROM.

Step 1. Data Capture

Text. For capturing text in machine-readable ASCII codes, a number of techniques can be used. If the text already is in machine-readable form on a personal computer, microcomputer, word processor, or typesetting system, the data can be transferred to the computer system which will be used for this (and perhaps other steps) of data preparation. If the text is not already in standard ASCII code (e.g. EBCDIC), it should be converted to ASCII.

If the text is not already in machine-readable ASCII, the text needs to be keyboarded or scanned using an Optical Character Recognition (OCR) reader. If the text must be in a symbolic (not raster) digital form, only OCR-type of scanners (versus image scanners) can be used.

At this stage, any inconsistencies in spelling variations, generic tags, etc., as well as typing errors should be eliminated, so the text data is consistent and accurate.

Images. Line art, photographs and other graphic images are digitized using a raster scanner. The scanner (digital camera) breaks the image into picture elements (pixels) which are expressed digitally. The number of lines per inch vertically and horizontally by which the image is broken will determine the number of pixels required for each square inch of the image.

Video Images. Video images are captured and broken into digital representation according to broadcast specifications (NTSC, PAL, SECAM, etc.). Each video image presented according to NTSC's specifications calls for 756 x 480 pixels. The CD-ROM can hold up to 9,000 of these 'still' video images. Video motion sequences (consisting of 30 images per second) use up 30MB of digital storage for one second. Thus, despite the large storage capacity of CD-ROM, it can only hold 5 to 6 minutes of video motion sequences.

To convert the analog signals of a video image to digital data, special decoders are used. The decorder may be contained in a special processor or digital video camera.

Audio. Audio recording equipment is used to enhance and convert analog signals into digital representation.

Step 2. Determining File Structure

This step, as discussed in the previous pages, is an important part of the CD-ROM. An existing file structure or specially-developed file structure may provide the best access to data. For some CD-ROM products, a file structure and naming conventions that can be used with a variety of operating systems allows the publisher to use disc contents in different markets and/or applications.

Step 3. Data Enhancement

At this point, the file structure is applied to the data, breaking files into logical sections if necessary and adding a common set of file identifiers

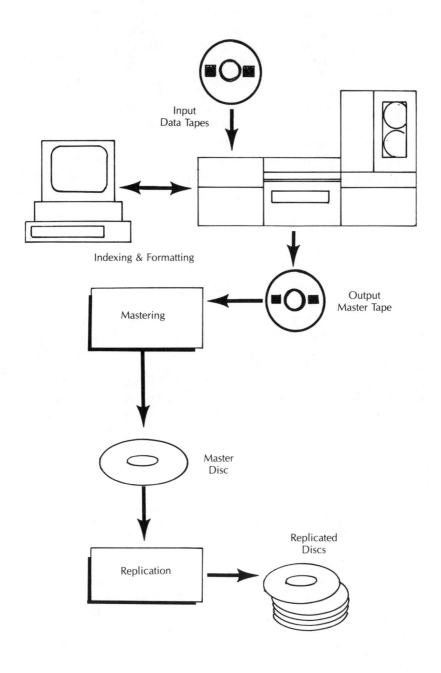

Input
Data Tapes

Indexing & Formatting

Output
Master Tape

Mastering

Master
Disc

Replication

Replicated
Discs

FIGURE 25:

CD-ROM Production Flow

FIGURE 26:

Digitizing Images

The amount of storage required for a digitized version of a graphic image depends on the scanning resolution. At 200 dots per inch (horizontally and vertically), an 8.5″ by 11″ image equals 3.74 MB of pixels. Using digital image compression techniques, the image can be stored in 0.5 MB. Using a higher resolution (400 dpi, for example) the image contains 14.9 MB of pixels. With compression, the image at this finer 'mesh' would require 2 MB of storage.

For continuous tone photographs, output from digitized storage does not necessarily show a dramatic difference in detail or resolution to the naked eye, even if the photographs were input at different dpi levels. The contrast might be similar in effect to the differences perceptible in two halftone screen gradations, such as those reproduced above.

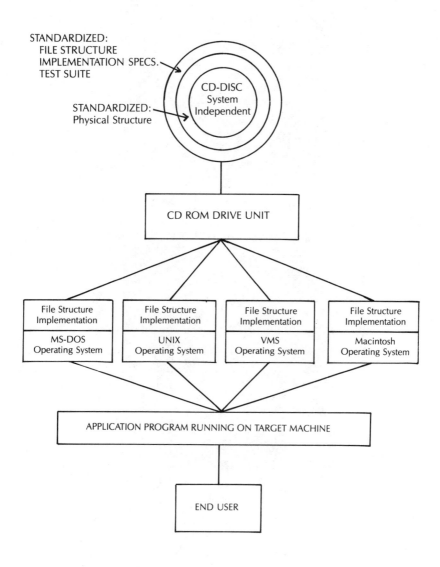

FIGURE 27:

Standard File Structures

A general purpose file structure is designed to allow the CD-ROM's database to be accessed in a variety of disc operating systems commonly used on microcomputers.

(including the name, size, type of file—audio, video, or text/digital codes).

Reference markers and stopword identifiers are incorporated into the text. Both of these will be used in subsequent steps of the production process.

Existing typesetting codes or generic markup codes in the text may be useful in locating logical file breaks and reference markers. Standardized markup—which identifies elements within the text and to which typographic codes may (or may not) be applied during composition)—is, of course, preferable over typesetting codes. In fact, standards[7] endorsed by the Association of American Publishers (AAP) were designed for just such situations where the text will be used for CD-ROM publishing, electronic publishing as well as print publishing.

Any remaining extraneous codes (e.g. typesetting codes, word processing commands, etc.) should be stripped.

Data Compression. Another aspect of the data enhancement process is eliminating any redundant or unnecessary data which would otherwise take up space on the disc and/or slow down retrieval time. Different data compression techniques exist for text and digitized images.

Textual data compression techniques include word replacement (with binary codes or abbreviations); substring replacement (similar to word replacment); stopword lists (eliminating words that have little content meaning); consecutive blank run length encoding; character bit compactions; and, for fielded data, eliminating embedded explanatory text and reinsert text only for display or printing.

Image data compression techniques include bit sampling, elimination of contrast levels, run-length encoding, Fourier analysis and other sophisticated schemes to represent the image accurately but not at the individual pixel level. Even after data compression, storage requirements for an 8 ½" x 11" image can be 50 to 500 times larger than text (an ASCII file) of an 8 ½" x 11" page.

At the end of Step 3, the data is 'clean', containing only data which will be information files and identification information about each file.

Step 4. CD-ROM Layout

Exactly how data is to be physically arranged on the CD-ROM is determined at this point. Based on the nature of the prepared database and the anticipated uses of the CD-ROM, files will be place sequentially along the spiral track, mapped to various sectors on the disc track, or interleaved with other files.

---

[7] Standardized Generalized Markup Language (SGML) was developed over several years by the GCA for the purpose of electronic markup. AAP's set of generic tags—to identify components of a document, such as chapter head, footnote, tables, etc.,—is derived from SGML. AAP urges the use of generic tags regardless of the input device used (word processor, PC, typesetting system, et.al.) and intended output device.

During this step, final decisions about how to reference (locate) data file contents will also be made as well as what retrieval software will be used. The position of the necessary 'locator' files (directories, indexes and/or hash algorithm tables[8] will also be determined.

The challenge of layout design is to, as much as possible, optimize access time without creating a locator scheme that is difficult or ineffective for the user or the application(s) of the database.

Step 5. Indexing

Files may be accessed through the use of a traditional file directory which contains a master listing of all files in the Database or CD-ROM. In many applications, the user wishes to see a specific part of the file, rather than starting at the beginning of the file.

To avoid searching in a linear fashion through the contents of a file to locate desired information, an indexed representation of the database can be created. This index also reduces the number of 'seeks' which must be made to obtain the desired data, thus enhancing system performance.

Indexing (also known as *text inversion*) builds a list of every word in the database marked as searchable and not on the stopword list and notes its location on the CD-ROM. Special inversion programs automate this process. However, due to the sheer volume of the database, text inversion may require breaking the database into sectons for indexing (and later remerging) unless a high-performance system with sufficient magnetic storage capacity is used.

Another means of locating data within files is the use of hash algorithm tables. These tables may supplement the index or, for some applications, replace the index.

Indexes can be almost as large as the initial database. Normally a 100% overhead is anticipated to allow sufficient disc space for both the database and the index.

Step 6. Testing with Application Software

In actual use of the CD-ROM, the index works in conjunction with the retrieval and application software. Therefore, once the indexing is complete, various testing is performed.

Simulating the CD-ROM layout, high-speed tests are performed using the retrieval software. Any problems in disc layout may alter the layout technique used, or the positioning of selected files. Other tests check the accuracy and completeness of the indexing. Still other tests check the suitability of one or multiple retrieval programs. Testing of the user interface (screen menus designed for the application, search argument prompts, etc.) is also performed.

---

[8] Hash algorithm tables are a means to both distribute data and to locate data on a disk. The tables consist of mathematical formulae, which show the location of data.

Problems uncovered during testing are corrected prior to proceeding to the next step.

Step 7. Premastering

Premastering is a term used for the process of creating a final magnetic tape version of the CD-ROM. A final file directory is created in CD-ROM format. The contents of all files are sequenced (each block of 2,048 bytes of data) according to sector position along the CD-ROM's spiral track.

During premastering, the additional 24 bytes of synchronizing codes, the header codes (sector address and mode indicator) and the error-checking codes are added to each block of data. Thus, all the data is in the CD-ROM data format. (Note: the conversion of data to CD-ROM sector format may optionally be performed by the disc manufacturer during the mastering process).

Beginning of Tape (BOT)	Reflective strip at beginning of tape
Volume Label (VOL1)	Identifies the volume
File Header 1 (HDR1)	Identifies the file and its sequence
File Header 2 (HDR2)	Contains basic file format information
Tape Mark (TM)	End of file mark
File Section	Contains user data
Tape Mark (TM)	End of file mark
File Trailer Labels (EOF1, EOF2, EOV1,EOV2)	Describe and delimit files. When a file is continued, EOV labels are written instead of EOF labels.
Tape Mark (TM)	Indicates the logical end-of-volume.
Tape Mark (TM)	Two consecutive tape marks must be written after the trailer labels of the last file on a volume.

FIGURE 28:

The ANSI standard (ANSI X3.27-1978) for Labelled Magnetic Tape

The final part of premastering is transferring the data onto magnetic tape. CD-ROM manufacturers request that premaster data tapes be standard ½ inch, 9-track mag tape and conform to the ANSI standard (ANSI X3.27-1978) for labelled magnetic tape.

Step 8. Mastering

The premaster data tapes are read into a computer where the data, once in CD-ROM sector format, is converted into the channel bits for each frame.

The channel-bit data drives an online master cutter. The cutter etches the channel-bits as microscopic pits and land (flat) areas along a tiny spiral track on a glass master disc. A laser, working from the center of the disc, exposes a photoresistant coating on the glass master.

This writing process takes place in real time, which would be too slow for volume replication. Instead, injection molding is used for replication. For the injection molding process, additional generations are necessary (positive-original, negatives, then multiple positives). To create these, the surface coating of the glass master is transferred onto a shell of nickel. That shell is used to create a negative impression onto several other shells. Those shells are subsequently used to create multiple CD-ROMs (positives).

Step 9. Testing

Before the negative shells are used, they are checked with special equipment to assure no errors or imperfections have been introduced. The contents of both the original and the 'negatives' are compared electronically.

Step 10. Manufacturing

This and other aspects of the manufacturing process demand high-quality precision equipment and special 'clean' environments. During manufacturing, the 'negatives' are used with injection molding techniques to create CD-ROMs. The newly-formed CD-ROMs are first covered with a reflective aluminum coating (for reading by the laser beam within the CD-ROM drive), then a protective lacquer coating.

The finishing process includes labelling, punching the center hole, and a series of quality control tests (some of which are performed by a laser scanner).

Production Time and Costs

The process of creating a CD-ROM product can, like any publishing project, span several months. The later portion of a CD-ROM publishing cycle (Steps 8-10) requires few days (on rush basis) or 2 weeks or several weeks (if the discs are not manufactured in the North America).

data should be logically referenced and ways users wish to locate data. That talent may be important to determining file structure, disc layout, indexing, etc. Similarly, firms knowledgeable in preparing data for print publishing may be quite helpful in data enhancement and preparation. In yet other cases, software development firms working in conjunction with hardware integrators may develop the better combination of hardware and software for a given application. In circumstances where the user system hardware is already established, hardware integrators aren't needed, yet the software integrators must be knowledgeable in the working of the CD-ROM system hardware. Obviously, required publishing services and their relative importance vary substantially, depending on the product to be published and the publisher's experience/expertise in CD-ROM publishing.

CD-ROM Publishing Systems

Initially all CD-ROMs were developed on custom systems. As the demand for CD-ROMs grows, systems for selected CD-ROM publishing tasks are becoming available. Thus a publisher or a provider of publishing services can purchase systems and/or software to perform selected steps in CD-ROM creation. Systems may be quite elaborate, running on dedicated minicomputers, with multiple perpherials for data conversion, enhancement, indexing and sequencing of text, images, video and audio. Or the CD-ROM publishing system may be small (PC-based) with custom programs for data preparation.

To illustrate, one PC-based system, called Bluefish (from Computer Access Corporation) offers the means to use unstructured, full-text files to build indexes and databases. The indexing and full-text management software allows the user to build, edit and search corporate, personal, or to-be-published databases. Once the database is constructed, quick access to data is possible on a PC, or internal MIS system. The database can also be used in the process of developing access from commerical online services or a CD-ROM.

Another PC-based system, called CD-Publisher (from VideoTools, Inc.), is targeted to the CD-ROM market. The system can perform the indexing (text inversion) and testing steps. At an IBM-PC/AT, clean, enhanced ASCII text files are input via PC floppy disks or magnetic (9-track, ½ inch) tape. Using its special software, it creates the index. Another (optional) software package (running on mini or mainframe) tests the index and sequences all the data, (by 2K of user data), according to the file structure and design layout scheme. The system will also add the additional coding and expansion of data into the final CD-ROM data format. A publisher or publishing service using this system would submit the data on magnetic tape to a mastering service.

A Multimedia Data Preparation System

A system for data preparation may be as basic as a microcomputer workstation, with magnetic tape drives (for reading in and writing out tapes), online magnetic storage, and data preparation software. The shaded items reflect those additional peripherals needed to capture video images in digital form and to convert audio analog signals into digital signals.

Source: The New Papyrus

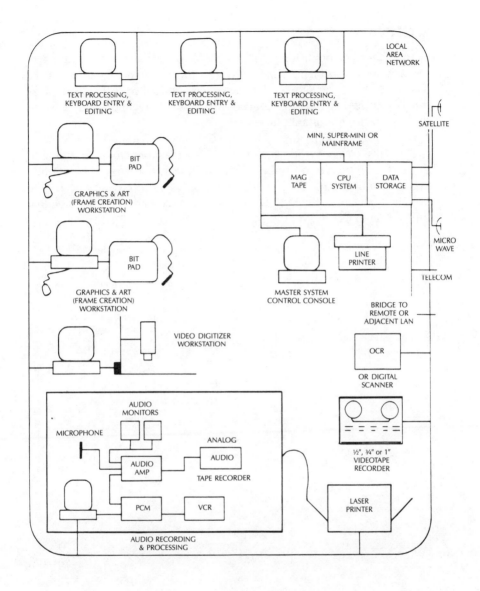

FIGURE 30:

A Data Creation, Capture, and Preparation System

A more elaborate system would also provide the means to create various materials, convert all materials (audio, video, graphic and text) into digital form, format and sequence the digital information, create a premastered version, test it, and generate the premaster magnetic tape.

Source: The New Papyrus

69

SECTION SUMMARY

The CD-ROM publishing process requires special expertise and systems, as does the print publishing process. The disc creation may be part of a larger project of developing special systems and software for the application of the CD-ROM. For larger projects, system integrators and software developers are important players.

In all projects, expertise in the special data preparation for CD-ROM materials is necessary. Some steps in data preparation are quite similar to those steps required in print publishing. In fact, data from a typesetting system can be used in the production process. Systems are just becoming commercially available to deal with those aspects of data preparation that are unique to CD-ROM publishing.

THE FUTURE:
CD-ROM'S and YOURS

Publishing on CD-ROM is still a new phenomenon. The technology has existed (in various forms) for several years. With the rapid adoption of CD-Audio has come, in the last three years, mass production facilities, consumer awareness of compact discs (in some form), and excitement about the distribution of other types of data in this compact form.

The interest in CD-ROMs and the CD-I variation is high. The technology works. The potential benefits are tangible. Its advantages are many—low distribution costs; significant space savings, compact/removable/transportable mass storage, re-usable data, durability, permanence, and rapid random access to large volumes of stored data. Yet the focus is primarily still on the technology, rather than its application. Perhaps it is a function of our 'high tech' environment. But how often do users explore the technology first? Our use of other distribution techniques—television, radio, records, video tapes, telephone communications, online services, even periodicals and books—rarely involves understanding *how* it works. We are, instead, focused on how well the technique fits our information needs, how convenient it is to use and how much it costs to use. To date, CD-ROM is still a technology-driven, not market-driven phenomenon.

The desired 'mass demand' for CD-ROM products will only be achieved when an individual can easily judge the value of a CD-ROM information system.

Reports on the potential for CD-ROM (usually expressed in terms of future dollars that will be spent on CD-ROM systems, drives, and discs) are based on selecting some collection of applications, estimating the total number of users currently interested—to any extent—in the subject-matter, and then extrapolating from those numbers the size of the market in some future year. Such projections are, of course questionable—especially when developed by those focused on technology, not user issues.

We won't insult the reader by presenting such projections that do not consider, for example, why CD-ROM (and not other optical media or floppy disks or online services or printed material, etc.) will be the 'proper' or only distribution technique for a given application. As we have already noted, in many cases, the CD-ROM form of distribution may complement, rather than replace, other means of information delivery. Instead we will point out factors which will impact the future of CD-ROM.

FACTORS AFFECTING THE FUTURE OF CD-ROM

Creative Uses of the Media

As with any new form, the challenge is creative use, not technical wizardry (which should be transparent to the user). CD-ROM offers the ability to package information—logically, randomly, and with audio and/or visual aids. We have already seen with some existing discs, such as the GEODISC (of mapping data) which supply specialized data in a form that is immediately of value to the end user. Likewise, the 'sound' library offers to its users a wide range of data in a form that is meaningful.

Thus, there are applications where CD-ROM is the only practical or most convenient information delivery system.

The MultiMedia Encyclopedia demonstration disc also illustrates several ways CD-ROM can be creatively used. Information—packaged as text with audio, text with images which can be enlarged, text with motion sequences, visuals with information expressed audibily, etc.—can enhance understanding, make the learning/information gathering process more enjoyable and effective, make information tasks less intimidating, and provide active (versus passive) feedback to the user.

Creative use of the media, rather than replication of other existing information forms, allows potential developers to work with, not in conflict with, other distributors and information providers with a common mission of serving the information user.

Perhaps most importantly, creative use also helps the user to see CD-ROM products as an effective, unique delivery mechanism and not solely in terms of a replacement for more familiar information delivery techniques.

Having the Necessary Equipment to Use CD-ROM

To use a CD-ROM requires (as a minimum) a microcomputer, interface, and CD-ROM player/drive.

If equipment is not already in place, the user has a substantial investment before a CD-ROM can be used. To obtain a system, the user must feel the system will be useful over time (unless the one disc program is so compelling the user assumes no other use for the system). Will just one disc justify the cost? (Who buys a television for just one show?) Or does the user need to know several discs can be used on the system? (Who buys a compact disc player for one recording?) And does the user need to know more than one company can supply discs? (Who buys a phonograph to play records from only one company?) At the consumer level, the user most often will need to know the number of CD-ROMs that will work on the system. Without standards, the likelihood of using the system for a variety of information programs from multiple publishers/information providers is questionable. (See information box for a discussion of the current state of standards for CD-ROM).

STANDARDS FOR CD-ROM

Whenever components (hardware and/or software) are developed by different groups or companies, characteristics of one or more components can limit or disallow the components to work together.

Certain incompatibilities among already existing, installed components won't go away. So various techniques are used to deal with the problems. Sometimes the incompatibilities are reduced by modification (such as adding a microchip and software patch to a microcomputer to get around the 32,000-byte maximum size for an MS-DOS file). Other incompatibilities require the development of interfacing devices and programs. Examples in the CD realm include using an SCSI or other interface to link the disc drive to the microcomputer.

When products and software are in the initial stages of development, the opportunity exists to establish a set of specifications (or standards) so components (regardless of origin) will work together. For Compact Disc technology, standards exist for certain aspects and efforts are underway to develop specifications for other aspects.

WHAT STANDARDS EXIST NOW

Existing standards for Compact Discs were jointly developed by Philips and Sony. These specifications, known as the Philips/Sony World Standard for Compact Discs, assure that CDs can be played on drives from different manufacturers. There are 3 sets of these standards: the Red Book (for CD-Digital Audio), the Yellow Book (for CD-ROM), and, under development, the Green Book (for CD-Interactive).

The standards spell out certain required functions of the drives (such as rotational speed, reading mechanism tolerances, synchronizing method, error detection and error correction, etc.). They also establish standard disc dimensions for a CD and other physical media characteristics, including:
■ Track and sector layout and data density
■ Content area of each sector, including method of addressing sectors
■ Error checking encoding to detect and correct reading errors

WHAT STANDARDS DON'T EXIST

The existing standards address physical properties of CD media. They do not specify:

- What file structure to use (to coincide with a microcomputer's disk operating system)
- How files should be laid out (distributed among sectors)
- What search/retrieval software to use.

For a common application, standards (or recommended programs) for disc layout and search/retrieval software may be possible. Both aspects are directly linked to the intended uses of the data and the disc content. Except for a specific application requiring multiple discs of similar content, to standardize these aspects could restrict CD-ROM performance and user-friendliness unnecessarily. Varying disc content and uses of the data requires different layouts and searching strategies.

Most of those involved in developing further standards don't necessarily want standards for disc layout or search/retrieval software. They do want a uniform filing structure. This would allow a user to use the CD-ROM with any microprocessor running a popular disk operating system (VMS, UNIX, MS-DOS and CP/M). (Consider how nice it would be to take a floppy disk with data stored on your IBM-PC, running MS-DOS, and *without* running a conversion program, be able to read the disk on another device running on UNIX or CP/M).

The lack of standards translates to extra development effort, cost, and required expertise on the part of the CD-ROM publisher. If/when standards are agreed upon, the publisher has at least one less decision to make in the production process (choosing and/or developing a file structure for a CD-ROM). With a file structure standard, the publisher can save the time to determine and design a file structure and would not have to create different CD-ROM versions to coincide with different operating systems. Currently, different versions are necessary if a CD-ROM publisher anticipates creating a disc that is intended for markets and applications where users already operate a variety of microprocessors (using various operating systems).

At least five different groups are known to be working on standards for CD file structure (also referred to as 'logical' disc structure).

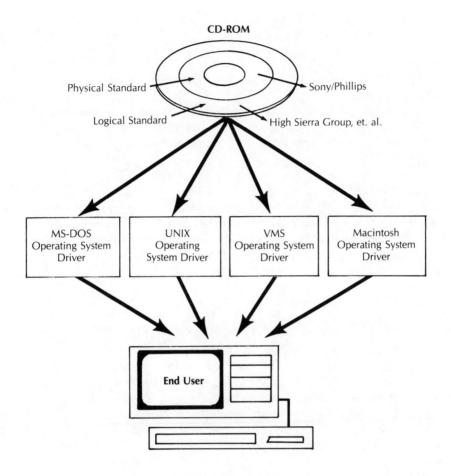

FIGURE 31:

Standardization of CD-ROM logical file structures allows the use of an existing or preferred system.

If equipment is not in place for the business user, the importance of standards (i.e. acquiring a 'standard' or generic system rather than a 'non-standard' system) depends on the needs of the information user. One disc, or multiple discs from one supplier, might adequately answer the user's needs—hence the custom nature of a system may not be relevant.

When some equipment, usually a microprocessor, is already in place[10], the ability to use that equipment as part of the information system is highly

---

[10] A study by Compact Discoveries, described at the Meckler Publishing Conference (December, 1985) on Optical Information Systems, looked at the installed base of personal computers. The survey of retail PC sales indicates that 36% of PC sales are to large companies and that 28% are to small businesses. Only 23% are sold into home environments.

desirable. Then the user has to add only the necessary additional components. Not only is the initial 'buy-in' less, the user already has some comfort level with using a computer. Thus, the user's potential 'computer-reticence' is reduced. The majority of existing CD-ROM systems work with IBM-PCs and compatibles, the more prevelant microcomputers used in businesses today.

But what of consumer/home markets, where fewer microprocessor are installed and more non-IBM products are used (such as Apple, Texas Instrument and Radio Shack)? To address the differences in number of installed microcomputers and likely uses for CD-ROM products in the home/consumer markets and business markets, attempts at developing 'standard systems' are underway. Part of this process is the development and differentiation of CD-I from CD-ROM. Since the CD-I player functions as a standalone drive (with the necessary computer programs resident or readable from the CD-I disc into the player's microchip), the user won't need a personal computer to use the CD-ROM technology.

Lower Costs for the User

CD-ROM potentially offers the user lower costs in three ways:

1. *Less money for the information itself.* If the user can acquire needed information for less money via CD-ROM than through other means, the user may prefer CD-ROM. If, on the other hand, the user feels only a portion of the disc's database is relevant to the user's specific information needs, the cost of the disc may be more than the cost of alternative information delivery systems. For example, why spend more than the cost of one magazine subscription to get a collection of magazines one doesn't read or need to reference? If the user is interested only in certain sections of a magazine, why not, instead, build a collection (on CD-ROM) that contains several years worth of sections or other publications the specialize in matters related to that topic, which—as a collection—costs less than the user would otherwise have to spend to obtain the data?

The implication for CD-ROM publishers will be to use the space on the disc wisely to package collections of data targeted to the user's needs.

2. *Lower space costs.* Another user cost is storing information. One of the reasons early CD-ROM projects have addressed the library market is the premium that market obviously places on shelfspace. In business, floor space for filing cabinets, shelves and deskspace is also expensive. Even more dramatic are those special environments where additional shelfspace is not a viable option, such as on a submarine, a space station, or mobile military unit (where service manuals, maps, etc. are needed).

3. *Lower access cost.* The third 'lower cost' implication relates to the time it takes to access data. All too often, a user must sift through stacks and reams of reference materials to locate information. The search may be for previously-seen information or for information the user hasn't specifically

seen but thinks may be contained in certain reading stacks, bookcases, files, etc. The lost time (and frustration) in seeking the data is expensive.

Convenience and Completeness

The need-to-get-all-the-facts quotient is a function of time, costs, and convenience. Who among us hasn't, at some point, decided that it just wasn't 'worth' the extra time, extra cost, or extra effort to 'dig deeper'?

The level of need quotient is sometimes determined by the information seekers. Other times other people (management, group members, clients, customers) set the level. In either case, the more convenient it is for the user to locate the facts, the more likely the user will obtain the right facts and not exclude important facts. Even if the costs are lower, even if the equipment is in place, even if the desired data resides on CD-ROM, the user must perceive the CD-ROM (and its system) as a convenient (or most convenient) method to get all the necessary facts.

While the relative importance of convenience in the need-to-get-all-the-facts equation can vary significantly in different work and personal situations, convenience is always part of the equation. To illustrate, let's consider two personal situations where the importance of convenience varies with time and costs. Prepared frozen food usually costs more than buying the fresh food and preparing it. But the convenience and time values in the 'need equation', for most of us, overshadow the additional costs. The further time-savings potential of microwave ovens in the preparation of frozen foods points out variations—among the same users—in the 'need equation'. Some frozen food users quickly purchased microwaves—due to the high premium placed on time or a fascination with new technology. Restaurants in particular, where the time-savings could be directly related to consumer satisfaction (and profits), were early adopters of the technology. Until the cost of microwave ovens came down, some frozen food users were unwilling to pay the additional amount for faster food preparation (i.e. time savings). Other frozen food users waited until frozen food packages included microwave instructions, microwave cookbooks or friends described the further conveniences possible. In other words, some frozen food users waited until they could gauge how convenient a microwave would be in their normal routine of food preparation.

The first four factors in adoption of CD-ROMs focused primarily on end-user issues. Just as important are factors for those who might invest in creating a CD-ROM as a provider.

Lower Costs for the Information Provider

Especially in business, the decision to use one information delivery system over another may reside at a managment level, not individual user level. Here, the cost-savings potential (versus convenience or time-savings) is most tangible. One manufacturer decided to use CD-ROM as the means to distribute service manuals based on the lower costs of CD-ROM versus printed materials. A 500-page service manual, containing over 5,000 illustrations, could be reproduced at a cost of $5.00 per CD-ROM and distributed to hundreds of locations for less than 50 cents. To reproduce the manual in printed form, the paper cost alone exceeded $5.00 per book and distribution costs would be significantly higher. The additional CD-ROM production costs are more than recovered in the lower reproduction costs.

Corporate publishers (unlike commercial publishers) can compare the total spectrum of costs, including corporate investment in equipment, CD-ROM publishing expertise and costs versus savings potential in time savings, accurate information dissemination and retrieval, space requirements, etc. For the commercial publisher, lower manufacturing costs are possible, too. But that lower cost may not be directly passed on to the end user. The publisher's other publishing expenses (besides manufacturing) and the commercial value of the information must be considered in establishing a selling price for the information on a CD-ROM.

Newness and Difficulty of Creating CD-ROM Programs

Another factor influencing the future of CD-ROMs is the impact that publishing information in this new medium has on the publisher. New expertise is required. New suppliers are probably involved. New options and considerations exist. Even if disc contents are limited to text and graphics, new design aspects come into play. With the addition of sound, audio, and interactivity, even more complex design issues enter the picture. And, heaven knows, a new world of terminology must be learned. The publisher will require, at the very least, staff members who become conversant about the issues and implications of CD-ROM publishing. These staff members will have to work with experts (newly hired in-house personnel or outside suppliers) in one or more areas: systems integration, CD-ROM-related hardware, software development, search and retrieval systems, computer graphics, CD-ROM design, data preparation, CD-ROM mastering and manufacturing, interactive instruction and program development, audio, and video. All in all, the process can be overwhelming!

Full-service companies and experts in selected aspects can (and have) minimize the newness and difficulties of creating CD-ROMs. Yet a publisher must still face a learning curve, with its associated costs and dangers. As more publishers have experience in CD-ROM publishing, other publishers will have a better grasp of what's involved, what pitfalls can be avoided, etc.

Influence and the Role of Vendors

Presently CD-ROM activities revolve around two types of organizations: suppliers of CD-ROM software/systems and suppliers of CD-ROM services. A third player (in a supporting, rather than starring role in most situations) is the publisher of CD-ROM discs. The suppliers of CD-ROM systems and services obviously make their money when they convince someone to develop a CD-ROM program/system. It is usually up to that 'someone' (publisher) to then sell the CD-ROM within an existing (e.g. corporate, professional information network) structure or to a group of potential users. Missing from the scenario is the groundswell of users, demanding the technology, per se.

As long as the CD-ROM activities revolve around the needs of CD-ROM suppliers and not the needs of the publishers and users, the future of CD-ROM is difficult to predict. Worse, while the CD-ROM suppliers cast about for the 'VisiCalc key'[11] for widespread adoption of CD-ROM, the focus of CD-ROM remains, inappropriately, at the supplier-technical level, not the user-application level. Until the role of CD-ROM suppliers becomes one of responding to publisher and user demand, rather than attempting to create demand, the adoption of CD-ROM as a information distribution medium will be limited.

This perception is in stark contrast to most speeches and published articles on the future of CD-ROM. Glowing comments abound, such as 'PCs and CD-ROMS—the marriage of the century', or from Mr. William Gates (president of Microsoft) 'In a few years, after the CD-ROM becomes commonplace, anyone looking back at the information, education and entertainment applications of today will understand the limited appeal they have had.' Not surprisingly, the sources, if not authorship, for CD-ROM articles and quotes are the CD-ROM suppliers themselves.

Based on the potential benefit of CD-ROMs, they will no doubt become a common means of information distribution. *None* of the factors affecting the future of CD-ROM suggest a demise of the medium. Rather they illustrate the difficulty in pinpointing when the demand for CD-ROM publishing will be commonplace.

IMPLICATIONS FOR THE PROVIDERS OF PUBLISHING SERVICES

With all this background, we can now address the relevancy of CD-ROM to you. The intended audience of this book are those people involved in the production of publications—printed, microfilmed, and/or online. As such, whether your organization is a commercial or in-house provider of publishing services, the role is to help the information provider prepare

---

[11] The 'VisiCalc key' refers to the phenomenally widespread adoption of personal computers resulting from the interest people had in using VisiCalc and other spreadsheet programs. The ability with VisiCalc to easily and automatically perform calculations and see the effects on various line items, was attractive enough to convince many people to buy a personal computer. Before the introduction of VisiCalc, the personal computer was used primarily by computer buffs or small special interest groups. A 'VisiCalc key' is a the means of unlocking a need or application so compelling that people will adopt the technology just to obtain this key.

materials for distribution. In that role, there are several implications of CD-ROM to consider.

Generic Copy Preparation

Interest and demand for generic, rather than typographic, coding of text will increase. As publishers consider CD-ROM and other media, they will need a generically-tagged version to edit, restructure, abstract and index materials. Some publishers will seek (or demand) the electronic version that was captured, prepared, and corrected, using such tags, rather than various word processed and composed versions. The preparer of the electronic composition version should be able not only to accept a generic-coded version of a manuscript, they may also need to provide the publisher with a generic version of the composed text.

Supplying Publishers with Digital Data

Previously-published materials needed in an anthology, for example, may already exist in electronic, digital form. If the only electronic version of the text exists on a composition system, the publishing service could compile (and if necessary modify) their files to help a publisher compile data in electronic form. Or the publishing service may provide expertise in conversion services to convert files existing on incompatible systems into a common database.

When the data is not in digital form anywhere, the publishing service could also help. The composition/publishing service may have the necessary resources (input operators for manual keyboarding or OCR devices) to convert textual material to digital form.

As more providers of publishing services also digitize graphics for electronic full-page composition, the expertise and equipment needed for scanning graphics may also be used to digitize images.

Expansion into New Publishing Services

Many providers of publishing services already offer additional services which would be valuable to CD-ROM publishers. For those who don't provide these additional services now, growing activity in CD-ROM publishing may suggest expanding their range of publishing services.

Some typesetters already offer data processing services, such as indexing, database management or database structuring of materials. For some applications, CD-ROM publishers will also need these services.

Some CD-ROM applications require the creation or use of slides. Those publishing services companies which already generate slides can also provide slide-design and slide-generation services to publishers needing slide images for a disc.

One of the most exciting uses for CD-ROM databases is the ability to store large amounts of material compactly and to generate hard copies only as necessary (versus printing, distributing and maintaining inventories). Typesetters and providers of publishing services could serve as the 'local node' in an information system, providing hardcopies on-demand for local distribution. Those who have already offered on-demand printing (via laser printers or typesetters) have found increasing interest in generating typographic-quality versions of documents. For CD-ROM-distributed documents, which could be quite complex and/or lengthy, the on-demand print order could be very large (in number of pages and/or number of copies needed). An agreement with even one corporation (versus multiple individuals with occasional on-demand needs) could be very lucrative.

Given the development of low-cost systems for CD-ROM data structuring, indexing and premastering, some providers of publishing services could expand their data preparation beyond print or online preparation to include CD-ROM data preparation. Especially when a publisher has already established a disc design, file structure, delivery system, etc., the disc creation process may not require involvement of system integrators, disc and software designers. Yet the publisher will need—for every disc—to prepare data. For typesetters and providers of publishing services who have specialized in preparing materials for one form a distribution, a logical expansion may be to include those data preparation tasks which are unique to CD-ROM.

Continuing to Serve the Publisher's Needs

The activities mentioned as 'expansion services' in the previous paragraphs could apply to both new, potential clients and existing clients. Especially for in-house providers of publishing services (and in varying degrees for commercial providers of publishing services), the most important implication of CD-ROM relates to the continuing ability and responsibility to serve their publishing clients. Even if a publishing service cannot offer expertise in CD-ROM production, it certainly knows a lot about production management, data capture and data preparation. That expertise could help a publisher (new to CD-ROM publishing) select outside services, determine the best way to digitize materials, etc.

Thus, even if the publishing service does not directly assume a production role, staff members could continue to help the publisher meet publishing goals. By serving in an advisory capacity or in a project managment role, the provider of publishing services can sustain the intended mission—helping the publisher control and complete publishing tasks.

Another Opportunity to Market Publishing Services

We have seen—with every new technological breakthrough and new product—a demand for documentation. Besides the technical documentation tied to development are the required parts manuals, catalogs, service and maintenance documentation, labels, warranties, packaging, training materials, reference guides, brochures, and promotional materials that accompany every product. Suppliers of CD-ROM hardware, software, full-service development, CD-ROM manufacturers as well as CD-ROM publishers have these documentation needs. Each of them is a prospect for typesetting services.

Answering Your Own Information Needs

You may well be using CD-ROM yourself. In addition to the Type Library collection, you may benefit from your own use of CD-ROM products or the use of a CD-ROM-based information system within your school system, at your library, your car dealership, your hardware store, your system supplier, even your attorney and your accountant.

FINAL SUMMARY

CD-ROM offers all of us a new method of distributing information. Its benefits are attractive not only to a publisher, but also to a user of information. Already informational professionals in selected fields, such as library and information services, are enjoying the benefits of CD-ROM.

The use of CD-ROM as a means of distributing information is just beginning. With the fast-moving pace of technological adoption today and the growing need for better information management, the future for CD-ROM is excellent.

Finishing this manuscript, with stacks, files and bookcases of information around me, I can hardly wait for the CD-ROM versions!

Rather than one more death toll for typesetting or printing, CD-ROM offers yet another opportunity to expand publishing services. Building upon already-established and needed expertise, providers of publishing services have much to offer the optical publishing industry.

REFERENCES

FOR FURTHER READING ABOUT CD-ROM

1985 Videodisc, Optical Disk, and CD-ROM Conference Proceedings. Edited by Roth, J.P., Meckler Publishing, Westport, CT. 1985.

Armstrong, A. 'New Lights on the Storage Front.' *Datamation.* September 15, 1985.

Barney, Ron. 'Betting on CD-ROM.' *Electronic Publishing Business.* Vol.5, May 1986.

Bowers, R.A. *The Optical/Electronic Publishing Directory.* Information Arts, POB 1032, Carmel Valley, CA 93924. 1986.

Bulkeley, W. M. 'Compact Disc Technology is Finding New Niches in Computer Data Field.' *Wall Street Technology.* November 1, 1985.

The CD-ROM/CD-I Puzzle: Where Do the Pieces Fit? Moses, Robert J. White paper. Philips Subsystems and Peripherals, Inc., New York, NY. May 1986.

CD-ROM: Dramatic Key to Information Dissemination and Use. Wilson-Cambridge, Cambridge, MA. 1985.

CD-ROM Market Opportunities Study. Market research report co-produced by LINK Resources and InfoTech. 1985.

CD-ROM Review, Premier Issue. DeTray, Jeff, editor. CW Communications, Petersborough, NH. 1986.

The CD-ROM Sourcebook. Helgerson, L.W. and Ennis, Martin, editors. Diversified Data Resources, Inc., Falls Church, VA.

CD-ROM Standards: The Book. Schwerin, J. et.al., jointly published by Learned Information Ltd. and InfoTech.

Essential Guide to CD-ROM. Roth, J. P., editor. Meckler Publishing, Westport, CT. 1985.

Foster, E., 'Grolier Puts Works on CD-ROM.' *InfoWorld.* July 29, 1985.

Gale, J. C. 'Use of Optical Disks for Information Storage and Retrieval.' *Informational Technology and Libraries.* 3, No.4. December, 1984.

Gale, J. C. 'The Information Workstation: A Confluence of Technologies Including the CD-ROM.' *Informational Technology and Libraries.* 2, No.4. June, 1985.

Jeffries, R. 'Goodbye, Gutenberg!' *PC Magazine.* November 12, 1985, pp.95-98.

The New Papyrus: CD-ROM. Microsoft Press, Richmond, WA. January 1986.

O'Connor, M. A. *'CD-ROM Versus Erasable Compact Disc.'* Videodisc and Optical Disk. 5, No. 6 (1985), pp. 454-460.

O'Connor, M. A. 'Application Development and Optical Media.' *Optical Information Systems* 5, No. 1 (1985), pp. 64-67.

Optical Information Systems. (Formerly *Videodisc and Optical Disk Journal).* Meckler Publishing, Westport, CT 06880.

Optical Memory's Impact on Magnetic Storage and Computer System Architecture. Electronic Trend Publications, 10080 North Wolfe Road, Suite 372, Cupertino, CA 95014. 1985.

Robertson, Barbara. 'See! See! CD-ROM' Computer Graphics World. July 1986, pp. 83-85.

Schwerin, J. B., 'Optical Publishing: Technological Breakthrough as a Marketing Challenge.' *Information Times* (Fall 1985), pp. 30-32.

Schwerin, J. B., 'Datext Targets Business Info Users with CD-ROM.' *Information Times.* (December 1985), pp. 1, 28.

Sheldon, Ken, editor. 'Mass Storage'. *Byte.* May 1986. pp. 159-246.

Taylor, Bruce A. 'Atlas Doesn't Shrug' *Computer Graphics World.* October 1986, pp. 46-48.

Technical Readings

All About the Compact Disc System. Sony Corporation, Sony Drive, Park Ridge, NJ. 1984.

Bardes, D'Ellen. 'Integration Tools Needed: Standards and Participation.' In *1985 Videodisc, Optical Disk, and CD-ROM Conference Proceedings.* Edited by Roth, J.P., Meckler Publishing, Westport, CT. 1985.

Free, J. 'The Laser-Disc Revolution.' *Popular Science.* May 1985, pp. 67-68, 107-110.

Hendley, T. 'Videodiscs, Compact Discs and Digital Optical Disks: An Introduction to the Technologies and the Systems and Their Potential for Information Storage, Retrieval and Dissemination'. Herts, Great Britain. Cimtech: The National Centre for Information Media and Technology. 1985.

Isailovic, J. *Videodisc and Optical Memory Systems.* Prentice-Hall, Inc. Englewood Cliffs, NJ. 1985.

Pohlmann, K. 'The Gutenberg Solution to CD-Making.' *Digital Audio.*(August 1985), pp.86-89.

Shuford, R.S. 'CD-ROMs and Their Kin'. *Byte.* November 1985, pp.137-146.

SOME COMPANIES INVOLVED WITH CD-ROM

This is a directory of selected firms active in CD-ROM systems, services and products. The appearance of one company, or the exclusion of another, should not be perceived as an endorsement (or condemnation) of their efforts. The intent of this list is to provide you with sufficient names to, if you choose, become more familiar with the companies and CD-ROM resources.

LEGEND

1 = Applications Developer	5 = Data Preparation	9 = Hardware Developer or Supplier	13 = Market Research
2 = Applications Software	6 = Disc Manufacturer	10 = On-Demand Printing	14 = Search & Retrieval Software
3 = CD-ROM Publisher	7 = Drive Manufacturer	11 = Premastering	15 = Systems Integrator/Developer
4 = CD-ROM Software	8 = Digitizing Services	12 = Publications	16 = Trade Associations

Firm Name	1	2	3	4	5	6	7	8	9	10	11	12	13	14	15	16
Academic Microbroadcasting Educational Network Dickinson TX	x														x	
Access Innovations Albuquerque NM			x													
Activenture Pacific Grove CA		x			x									x		
AllTech Communications Cincinnati OH															x	
Apple Computer Cupertino CA									x							
Aquidneck Data Corp. Middletown RI		x		x										x	x	
Automated Info Reference Systems College Park MD														x	x	
Battelle (Software Products) Columbus OH		x												x		
Borland International Scotts Valley CA		x														

85

Firm Name	1	2	3	4	5	6	7	8	9	10	11	12	13	14	15	16
Brodart Library Automation Div. Williamsport, PA			x													
Bowker Electronic Publ.			x									x				
Cambridge Scientific Abstracts Bethesda MD			x													
College Systems Integration Mission KS										x						
ComDisc Los Angeles CA						x										
Compact Discoveries Delray Beach FL	x	x		x	x									x	x	
Computer Access Belmont MA														x		
Cuneiform Systems Nashua NH	x	x		x	x				x					x	x	
Cytation, Inc. San Francisco CA	x	x	x		x											
DATATEK Oklahoma City OK			x													
Datext Woburn MA			x													
Denon America Fairfield NJ					x	x	x				x					
Destron Chicago IL																
Digital Audio Disc Corp. Terre Haute IN						x									x	
Digital Equip. Corp. Bedford MA	x															x

Firm Name	1	2	3	4	5	6	7	8	9	10	11	12	13	14	15	16
Digital Library Systems Rockville MD														X		
Disclosure Online Database Bethesda MD			X													
DOCdata NV Venlo, The Netherlands						X										
D & B Info. Systems Murray Hill NJ			X													
Earth View, Inc. Ashford WA		X													X	
Fairfield Research Darien CT													X			
The Faxon Co. Westwood MA			X													
Fulcrum Technologies Ottowa Ontario														X		
General Research Corp. Santa Barbara CA			X													
Geographic Data Technology Lyme NH			X													
GEOVISION Inc. Norcross GA			X													
Grolier Electronic Publishing New York NY			X													
Group L Herndon VA														X		
The H.W. Wilson Co. Bronx NY	X														X	
Hewlett-Packard Palo Alto CA															X	

Firm Name	1	2	3	4	5	6	7	8	9	10	11	12	13	14	15	16
Highlighted Data Washington DC					X										X	
Hitachi Sales Corp. of America Compton CA						X	X									
Image Conversion Techn. Burlington MA								X								
Information Arts Carmel Valley CA												X				
Info. Dimensions Inc. Dublin OH	X													X		
Info. Handling Services Englewood CO			X													
InfoTech Pittsfield VT													X			
In-Four Los Altos CA					X											
Interactive Video Systems Chicago IL	X															
Intl. Thomson Information Arlington VA	X	X			X											
Knowledge Access Los Altos CA	X			X	X											
LaserData Inc. Cambridge MA	X				X									X		
LaserVideo Chicago IL						X										
Library Association London England			X													
Library of Congress Washington DC			X													

88

Firm Name	1	2	3	4	5	6	7	8	9	10	11	12	13	14	15	16
The Library Corp. Washington DC			x	x	x									x	x	
LINK Resources New York NY													x			
Meckler Publishing Westport CT												x				
Micromedex Englewood CO			x													
Microsoft Press Bellevue WA				x								x				
microTRENDS Schaumburg IL									x							
Nat'l Decision Systems Encinitas CA			x													
Nat'l Technical Info. Sys. Springfield VA			x													
Newsbank/Readex New Canaan CT			x													
OCLC Inc. Dublin OH			x													
ONLINE Computer Systems Germantown MD	x				x										x	
Panasonic						x	x									
Philips Subsystems New York NY						x	x		x		x				x	
PolyGram GmbH Hannover West Germany						x										
Psyc. Abstracts Info Services Arlington VA			x													

Firm Name	1	2	3	4	5	6	7	8	9	10	11	12	13	14	15	16
Quantum Development Corp. Denver CO		x												x		
Reference Technology San Diego CA Dallas TX Vienna VA Westlake CA	x	x		x	x						x			x	x	
Rothchild Consultants San Francisco CA												x	x			
Scotch 3M Optical Recording Minneapolis MN Mountain View CA					x	x	x		x		x					
Sony Corporation Park Ridge NJ						x	x								x	
TMS, Inc. Stillwater OK	x	x			x						x			x	x	
UTLAS Corp. White Plains NY			x													
U S Geological Survey Reston VA	x	x											x	x		
Univ. Microfilm Ann Arbor MI			x													
VideoTools Aptos CA		x		x					x		x				x	
Wilson-Cambridge Cambridge MA	x	x			x										x	
XEBEC Sunnyvale CA			x						x							

90

GLOSSARY

A

ACCESS TIME A term than can be used to describe several types of computer memory or storage activities. (1) The time it takes for an instruction or unit of data in computer memory to get to the processing unit of a computer. (2) The time it takes a unit of data to get from a direct-access storage device to computer memory. (3) The time it takes a reading device to move to the proper position, read the data, and transmit the data to a computer processor.

ADDRESS A coded representation of the specific destination or location on a storage media. For CD-ROM, addresses of each sector on the disc are expressed as MM:SS:BB along the spiral track of the disc.

ALGORITHM A method of problem solving using a prescribed, finite set of well-defined steps. Algorithms are sometimes used to determine data destinations and locations on a CD-ROM.

ANALOG That which is continuously available (like a wave), rather than that which is discreetly variable (like pulses). Not digital (off/on), but continuous.

APPLICATIONS SOFTWARE Programs designed for specific user tasks, e.g., word processing, full-text search and retrieval.

ARTIFICAL INTELLIGENCE (AI) Computer programs that perform functions, often by imitation, which are normally associated with human reasoning and knowledge.

ASCII (American Standard Code for Information Interchange) The binary transmission code used by most teletypewriters and display terminals. Used in computers and communications systems to define each character or number by 8 bits (one byte) of digital code.

B

BANDWIDTH (1) The difference between the lowest possible and highest possible frequencies of a frequency band, expressed in cycles per second. (2) The width of a band of frequencies. Also used, informally, to represent the maximum number of information units (bits, characters) that can transverse a communication path per second.

BITS Contraction of the term 'binary digits' (zero and one). The smallest pieces of data recognizable to a computer.

BIT-STREAM Refers to a binary signal without regard to groupings of bits by character.

BIT STRING A group of arbitrarily arranged binary digits (bits).

BITS PER SECOND (BPS) A measure of transmission speed in information systems.

BLOCK ERROR CORRECTION A data recovery method to ensure recovery of all user data. Applied to the physical block of user data (2,048 bytes) during CD-ROM premastering.

BOOLEAN SEARCH A search strategy for expressing criteria for selecting information. The search request is stated with AND, OR, and NOT functions.

BUFFER A temporary storage device used to compensate for different rates of data flow or processing rates when data moves from one device or function to another.

BURST ERROR Errors detected in consecutive data bits.

BURST MODE A method of writing or reading data that does not permit an interrupt to occur.

BYTE A group of bits, processed or operating together. Used to describe one position or one character of information. The most common byte is 8 bits long.

C

CD A compact disc. Sometimes, informally used to refer to the CD-Audio disc.

CD-I Acronym for the Compact Disc-Interactive disc.

CD-ROM Acronym for the Compact Disc Read-Only Memory disc.

CHANNEL (1) A path or circuit along which information flows.(2) In television, a single path or section of the electro-magnetic spectrum that carries a television signal.

CHANNEL SEPARATION Gaps in the digital code stream to distinguish one series of signals from another.

CHARACTER STRING Any group of characters acted upon in a computer system as though they were a single unit.

CHECK BIT A single binary digit used to determine and express the status of a byte of data. Also known as a parity bit.

CIRCUIT A means of two-way communications between two points.

COMPACT DISC READ-ONLY MEMORY (CD-ROM) A 4.72-inch (12 cm) read-only optical memory disc based on the Philips/Sony World Standard that stores up to 600 megabytes of data.

COMPACT DISC PROGRAMMABLE READ-ONLY MEMORY (CD-PROM)
This type of compact disc can be written to only once by the user.

CONSTANT ANGULAR VELOCITY (CAV) The rotation of disc media (magnetic or optical) at a steady, non-changing number of rotations per minute.

CONSTANT LINEAR VELOCITY (CLV) Varying rotational speed of a disc so data is always passing the disc reading mechanism at the same rate of speed. To keep the data speed constant, the disc spins faster when the reading head is at the outer edge of the disc (500 rpm) and decreases rotational speed (down to 200 rpm) as the read head moves closer to the center of the disc.

CROSS-INTERLEAVED REED-SOLOMON CODE (CIRC) A sophisticated method of error detection and correction that involves techniques of data delay and data rearrangement. CIRC detects and corrects up to two errors in one code word and interpolates for long error bursts. Undetected errors using this technique are rated at one bit error in a trillion bits.

D

DATABASE (1) A collection of stored information. (2) A collection of digitally-stored data records. (3) A collection of data elements within records within files that have relationships with other records within other files.

DATA BUS Computer hardware that transmits coded data between processors or other hardware components in a computer system.

DATA COMPRESSION A technique that saves storage space, such as eliminating gaps, empty fields, redundancy or unnecessary dates, to shorten the length of records or blocks.

DATA FILE A set of related data in which all records are organized alike and which can be accessed under a single name.

DATAROM An acronym Sony uses for its 5.25-inch optical read-only memory disc. Also referred to as OROM.

DATA PREPARATION The procedure by which already existing data is converted from its present media into a form better suited for use on a CD-ROM.

DEVICE DRIVER Software telling the computer how to communicate with the CD-ROM drive.

DIGITAL AUDIO The storage of sound and music on a compact disc.

DIGITAL TO ANALOG CONVERTER Mechanical or electronic device used to convert digital numbers to continuous analog signals. Also referred to as a D-A Converter or DAC.

DISC An optical storage media.

DISK A magnetic storage media.

DISK OPERATING SYSTEM (DOS) A software program that controls the flow of data between a system's internal memory and external disks. Popular disk operating systems for micro and minicomputers are VMS, MS/DOS, CP/M, and UNIX. Examples of CD-ROM disc operating systems are Reference Technology's STA/File, TMS's LaserDOS, and Digital Equipment Corporation's Uni-File.

DRAW (Direct-Read-After-Write) A write-once recording technique for an optical memory disc or card, which verifies accuracy of the recording immediately after each portion of the media is written.

DRDW (Direct-Read-During-Write) Refers to the ability to read information during the writing/recording process.

E

EBCDIC (Extended Binary Coded Decimal Interchange Code) An 8-bit code used to represent numbers and characters. Developed by IBM and used primarily by IBM equipment.

EPROM (Erasable Programmable Read-Only Memory) Read-only memory in which data can be erased by ultraviolet light or other means. Data can be rewritten bit by bit with appropriate voltage pulses.

ERROR CORRECTION CODE (ECC) A method of data recovery used in reading and premastering CD-ROMs. Correction restores a single physical block of user data (2,048 bytes).

ERROR DETECTION CODE (EDC) A method of discovering errors, used in conjunction with ECC.

ERROR RATE The ratio of the amount of erroneously transmitted data to the total amount of data sent.

F

FRAME The smallest information unit on an optical disc, equal to 588 bits on a CD-ROM.

FILE STRUCTURE A logical method of organizing data into locations which can be quickly accessed.

G

GREEN BOOK The specifications under development for the physical characteristics of CD-I discs and players.

H

HARD READ ERROR Physical bits of data misplaced or missing from the data bit stream.

HASH ALGORITHM TABLES A means to both distribute data and to locate data on a disk. The tables consist of mathematical formulae, which show the location of data.

HIGH SIERRA GROUP A working group of representatives from various CD-ROM companies who are proposing a set of standards for CD-ROM beyond characteristics set forth in the World Standards established by Phillips and Sony.

I

INDEX A listing of words and their locations (addresses) on a disk/disc.

INTERACTIVE A term used in optical disc applications for describing the ability of the system to determine the next frame or sector of data to be presented based on the user response. Not serial, but random access.

INTERLEAVING (1) A multiprogramming technique in which parts of one computer program are inserted into another program so that if there are processing delays in one program, parts of the other program can be processed. (2) A method of intermixing data on an optical disc to reduce access time.

L

LAND The reflective area between two adjacent (non-reflective) pits on a CD-ROM surface.

LASER (Light Amplification by Stimulated Emission of Radar) (1) A device that transmits a narrow, coherent beam of electromagnetic energy. (2) The light source in an optical drive for reading data stored on an optical disc.

LASER/DOS TMS's operation system for a CD-ROM system.

LASERCARD™ Trademarked name for optical memory cards from Drexler Technologies.

LV-ROM An acronym for a videodisc consisting of digital data stored as analog signals

M

MASS STORAGE A device which can hold very large amounts of information cheaply with automated access on demand.

MASTER The original recording of a finished program.

MASTERING The process of producing a glass master disc from the premastered data stored on magnetic tape or disk. The master is used to create 'negative' copies used to replicate multiple copies.

O

OFF THE SHELF Professionally produced, pre-packaged programs; the alternative to custom-produced materials.

OPTICAL HEAD An assembly within an optical drive containing the components that reflect laser light on the data surface of the disc and covert the reflected light into electrical signals that can be interpreted as data. Components in the optical head are the laser, lenses, prisms, a focusing mechanism and a photodetector.

P

PERIPHERAL EQUIPMENT Supplementary equipment that puts data into or accepts data from a computer.

PIT The microscopic depression in the reflective surface of a CD-ROM.

PREMASTERING The conversion of user data into a format suitable for CD-ROM mastering and replication. In addition to adding error detection/correction codes, synchronizing, and header codes, data may be organized for placement on disc.

PROM (Programmable Read-Only Memory) A memory that is not programmed during manufacturing. To program, a physical or electrical process is necessary.

Q

QUERY LANGUAGE An alternative to conventional programming languages or structures that allows a user to create information retrieval requests without formal training in algorithmic thought/formulae.

R

READ (1) To acquire or copy data from one storage device/medium to another. (2) The opposite of write.

RED BOOK The specifications developed jointly by Philips and Sony for the physical characteristics of CD-Digital Audio discs and players.

ROM acronym for Read-Only Memory A semiconductor (circuit) that contains prewritten programs or data. The content of ROM circuits is permanent.

S

SECTOR The smallest addressable unit of a CD-ROM. Each sector contains 2,048 bytes of user data plus identifier, synchronizing codes, and error correction/detection codes.

SEEK To locate a sector on a disk/disc with the reading head of the disk/disc drive.

SEEK ERROR The disk drive's inability to locate a sector as a result of physical or mechanical problems like vibration, poor laser focusing, and disk/disc surface irregularities.

SERVO-MECHANISM Control systems which read their own output to determine the degree of further output needed. Servo-mechanisms are in optical disc drives to control the movement and functions of the optical (reading) head.

SIGNAL Visual or audio information converted into electrical impulses.

SMALL COMPUTER SYSTEM INTERFACE (SCSI) A standard 8-bit parallel interface frequently used to connect disk drives and other peripherials to a microcomputer.

STA/FILE Reference Technology Inc.'s operating system for a CD-ROM system.

SUBSTRATE A physical material on which a circuit is built. The base material for CD-ROM discs is a strong, transparent polycarbonate plastic.

T

TEXT INVERSION An automated process to extract from a database all words which should be referenced and their locations within the database.

TPI Shorthand for 'tracks per inch', a unit measure of a media's physical storage structure and capacity.

TRACK A groove within a storage disk/disc. On a CD-ROM is one continuous, tightly-coiled spiral track 3-miles long.

TRANSFER RATE The rate, usually expressed in bytes per second, at which information can be sent from one device or component to another. The transfer rate of a CD-ROM has been measured at 150,000 bytes per second.

TURNKEY SYSTEM An integrated configuration of preselected hardware and software designed to accomplish a particular processing task. A turnkey system is an alternative to developing, integrating, and testing all components of a system.

U

UNI-FILE Digital Equipment Corporation's operation system for a CD-ROM system.

V

VIDEO Pertaining to the bandwidth and spectrum position of the signal resulting from television scanning.

VTOC (Volume Table of Contents) The portion of a CD-ROM (or any other disk) containing basic labelling, including name of the disc, copyright data, volume number (if part of a larger set of discs), version number, pointers to data blocks, etc.

W

WORLD STANDARD refers to The Philips/Sony World Standards for Compact Discs. Three documents (the Red Book, Yellow Book and Green Book) describe physical characteristics of CD-type discs and players.

WORM (Write Once Read Many) acronym for a Write-Once optical medium which allows the user to write data once (permanently onto the medium) and to read data stored on the medium indefinitely.

Y

Yellow Book The specifications developed jointly by Philips and Sony for the physical characteristics of CD-ROM discs and players.

ABOUT THE AUTHOR

Patti Myers is president of Patti Myers & Associates, a consulting firm she established in 1978. The firm specializes in serving clients who have information processing and composition needs. These clients often have diverse and unique requirements which demand careful, individual analysis and evaluation to assure the most appropriate recommendations. For many clients, additional services are provided so that new procedures, processes and products are smoothly integrated within their existing environments.

After graduating with honors in English and psychology from The Ohio State University, Ms. Myers joined the VariTyper Division of AM International. She later joined Compugraphic Corporation where she held positions of national marketing manager for advanced systems and senior corporate planner.

Ms. Myers is a contributing editor to numerous industry publications and has previously written books for the National Composition Association. She is also a frequent speaker on topics and trends affecting publishers, corporate publishing operations, typographers and printers.

About The National Composition Association

The National Composition Association (NCA), founded in 1964, is a National Affiliate of Printing Industries of America, Inc. With over 700 active members and subscribers, NCA is the world's leading association for the prepress composition industry. When professionals need answers to questions on typography, digital imaging and composition equipment, productivity or marketing, they look to NCA.

Here are some of the many benefits and services available to NCA members, some of which are also available separately to NCA non-member publication-only subscribers (marked with an asterisk):

- Frequent new monographs, studies, and other publications ten to twelve times a year. First copy free.*

- *NewsLine,* the monthly newsletter.*

- *NCA Reports,* recurring updates and supplementals on industry trends and practical information for the typographer.*

- Annual Convention (held in conjunction with Type-X). Members can attend at a reduced rate.

- NCA conferences and seminars. Members can attend NCA's many conferences at a reduced rate.

- Listing in *Who Who's,* a directory of membership and type buyer's guide.

- Technical Inquiry Service, available to members.

- TypeLine, NCA's electronic bulletin board with proven and experimental software available for member downloading.

Write or call for more information.

National Composition Association
1730 North Lynn Street
Arlington, VA 22209
(703) 841-8165